THE TRUTH ABOUT TESTING

An Educator's Call to Action

W. James Popham

ASCD

Association for Supervision and Curriculum Development
Alexandria, Virginia USA

Association for Supervision and Curriculum Development
1703 N. Beauregard St. Alexandria, VA 22311-1714 USA
Telephone: 1-800-933-2723 or 703-578-9600 Fax: 703-575-5400
Web site: http://www.ascd.org E-mail: member@ascd.org

Printed in the United States of America.

November 2001 member book (pc). ASCD Premium, Comprehensive, and Regular
members periodically receive ASCD books as part of their membership benefits.
No. FY02-02.

ASCD Product No. 101030

ASCD member price: $19.95   nonmember price: $23.95

Library of Congress Cataloging-in-Publication Data
Popham, W. James.
    The truth about testing: an educator's call to action / W. James Popham.
        p. cm.
"ASCD Product No. 101030."
Includes bibliographical references and index.
  ISBN 0-87120-523-8 (alk. paper)
  1. Educational tests and measurements—United States.
2. Education—Standards—United States. I. Title.
  LB3051.P6145 2001
  371.26'013—dc21

                                        2001004701

06   05   04   03   02   01   10 9 8 7 6 5 4 3 2 1

The Truth About Testing

Acknowledgments

I WISH TO THANK THE EDITORIAL CREW AT THE ASSOCIATION FOR SUPERvision and Curriculum Development (ASCD), who invited me to write this book. John O'Neil was the ASCD editor who was most persuasive in encouraging me to write a book based on my own measurement-related experiences. ASCD asked me to draw on those experiences to identify how educational testing could help or harm classroom instruction. Although I encouraged the editors to title this book *W. James in Assessment Land*, they sensibly declined.

My appreciation also goes to ASCD for appointing a superb special-assignment editor, Robert W. Cole, who went through each of the book's chapters with a skilled editor's incisive insights, always offering corrective suggestions when he detected verbal folly. Bob's editing made the book much better. If you find what I've written less than entrancing, think of how dreary it would have been had Bob not spruced it up.

Once the completed manuscript had been sent to ASCD Central, Katie Martin and her plucky pack of editorial mavens gave it a more than meaningful massage. Two chapters were significantly reworked—and strengthened. I appreciate the hard work Katie and her crew put into making this a better book.

Finally, my thanks go to Dolly Bulquerin, friend and wordprocessing wonderwoman, who translated my hand-scratched symbols into something resembling sentences—many of which turned out to be grammatically correct.

Typically, at this point an author accepts personal responsibility for any of a book's shortcomings. As a change of pace, however, if you find anything you don't like in the book, blame John, Bob, Katie, or Dolly. I am completely innocent!

WJP
Kauai, Hawaii
June 2001

Introduction:
How We Arrived at
This Unhappy Place

THIS IS A BOOK ABOUT EDUCATIONAL TESTING IN THE UNITED STATES. Although its main focus is what people call *high-stakes tests*, much of the content also applies to the classroom assessments teachers routinely generate for their students.

I believe that today's high-stakes tests, as they are used in most settings, are doing serious educational harm to children. Because of unsound high-stakes testing programs, many students are receiving educational experiences that are far less effective than they would have been if such programs had never been born.

I also believe that most teachers are missing a major dividend that educational testing can provide. Teachers are failing to take advantage of the instructional benefits that *properly constructed* tests can bring to themselves and to their students. As I'm using the phrase, a "properly constructed" test is one that significantly illuminates the instructional decisions teachers must make. If all high-stakes tests were properly constructed, we'd find that a high-stakes testing program would typically have a positive effect on educational quality.

And that, in a nutshell, is what this book is about. It begins by addressing the current misuses of high-stakes tests, and then explains how we can create tests that can improve, not degrade, instructional quality. To ensure that I don't make any profound pedagogical mistakes, I suppose I should state this book's two objectives outright. After completing this book, I want you to

1. Understand the misuses of today's high-stakes tests and be able to explain to others what those misuses are and why they occur.

2. Recognize the distinguishing features of an instructionally illuminating test and be able to differentiate between tests that are and are not instructionally illuminating.

With respect to the second objective, I have no illusions that completing this slender volume will transform you into a measurement maven who, in scant inspired moments, can whip out a brand new test that will help teachers teach better and students learn better. No, that's a mite ambitious. (You'd probably need to read the book *twice* before you'd be up to that.) What I really want is for you to be able to review any high-stakes test currently being foisted on you (or a test that's under consideration for possible foisting) and confidently determine whether the test is apt to be—from an instructional perspective—a winner or a loser.

Throughout this book, I use the words *test, assessment,* and *measurement* in an essentially interchangeable manner. There are no special nuances associated with the three terms; all refer to a wide range of ways that educators can get a fix on a student's status. When I use any of the three synonyms, I am definitely thinking of more than paper-and-pencil tests of the traditional sort that most of us experienced as we went through school. Today, educational assessment includes a much broader, and sometimes quite nontraditional array of measurement approaches. You'll be reading about many of these newer ways of testing as you proceed through this book.

So that you understand from whence I'm coming regarding the book's content, let me give you a compressed look at my personal educational meanderings in a career spanning almost the entire last half of the 20th century. Interestingly, it was during this 50-year period that educational tests were transformed from teachers' tools into teachers' terrors.

In 1953, soon after I wrapped up my teacher education requirements, I took my first teaching job as a high school instructor in a rural eastern Oregon town. It was a small town—only 1,800 inhabitants—and I was delighted to be there . . . it was the only job offer I received.

Testing was regular practice in that Oregon high school. My colleagues and I built and administered all sorts of our own classroom tests. We even administered standardized achievement tests each spring. In retrospect, I believe our town's school superintendent insisted that standardized tests be given only because such tests were required in the larger Oregon school districts. Perhaps he saw them as a mark of cosmopolitan progress. We may have been rural, but as our superintendent once proudly proclaimed, "We use national tests!"

No one paid any real attention to our students' scores on those standardized tests. The citizens of our town thought we teachers were doing a satisfactory job. And for the most part, we were. On occasion, a few students failed to perform all that well in school, and some teachers were certainly less effective than others. But in general, the teachers in my high school (and in the town's elementary school) were thought to be successful. The children were learning, and parents were pleased.

That's pretty much the way it was throughout the United States at midcentury. Although there were surely some so-so teachers out there, it was generally believed that America's teachers were doing what they were being paid to do—and doing it pretty well.

After my high school teaching experience, which I really cherished, I picked up a doctorate focused on instruction from Indiana University. I taught in a pair of small colleges, and, in 1962, I joined faculty of the UCLA Graduate School of Education. My chief assignment at UCLA was to teach prospective teachers about instructional methods.

Even at that time—the early 1960s—confidence in public schools was generally quite high. One rarely heard heated attacks on the caliber of our national educational system. Although there were occasional books critical of schools, such as Rudolf Flesch's *Why Johnny Can't Read*, most citizens thought, as had their parents before them, that the nation's schools were very successful.

Faith Followed by Doubts

Since its earliest beginnings, public education has been regarded as one of the United States' finest accomplishments. Consistent with most people's conception of what a democratic society ought to be, our public schools have offered a toll-free road that can lead even the most humble to success, happiness, and a good life. Consider the starring role American public schooling plays in some our fondest patriotic metaphors: Public education is the latchkey that can open the door to a land of opportunity; it is the cornerstone of our nation's democratic system of government.

These sentiments capture the positive regard for public education, for teachers, and for the teaching profession itself that was widely held by most U.S. citizens well into the 1960s. Students were assumed to be learning, and teachers were assumed to be teaching. All was much as it should be.

But sometime during the late 1960s and early '70s, mutterings of public discontent began to surface. Newspapers published the first articles about students who had secured high school diplomas, yet couldn't fill out job application forms properly. Other scare stories hit the press about students who, although unable to read or write at even a rudimentary level, were being promoted merely on the basis of "seat time." U.S. public schools, long venerated, were coming under increasingly serious attacks. And, of course, this assault included the nation's teachers who, some said, had failed to teach America's children what those youngsters needed to know.

Minimum Competency Tests

Because widespread citizen distress often engenders some sort of legislative response, a number of state legislatures, as well as several state and district school boards, soon established basic-skills testing programs (usually focused on reading, writing, and arithmetic). New regulations required students to pass these tests before receiving their high school diplomas. In some instances, students in lower grades were obliged to pass a specified test before being promoted to the next higher grade. The policymakers who established these tests typically referred to such assessments as *minimum competency tests*. The objective, the policymakers claimed, was to supply parents with a "limited warranty" that a child who passed a competency test had *at least* mastered the fairly modest set of basic skills these tests measured.

But whether the tests' warranties were limited or not, they definitely made a meaningful difference to the students who failed them. Denying a diploma to a high school student on the basis of that student's score on a single test created a whole new set of rules for educational measurement. Penny-ante assessment was definitely over; high-stakes testing had arrived.

Although at first glance it would seem that the focus of the late-1970s minimum-competency tests was on students, this really wasn't the case. The policymakers who installed these competency tests were actually displaying their doubts about public school educators. As legislators and other educational policymakers saw the problem, if kids were making their way through an educational system without having learned how to read, write, or fill out a job application, then someone was falling down on the job—falling down on the job of *teaching*.

Not surprisingly, members of the business community lined up solidly behind the establishment of minimum competency testing programs. After all, corporate America needed high school graduates who possessed basic skills. And if competency tests could even partially guarantee that graduates possessed those skills, then corporate America quite naturally endorsed these tests with gusto.

Most of the minimum competency tests of the 1970s and early '80s focused on remarkably low-level skills and knowledge. The reason is worth considering. It's a lesson from which today's educators might profit as they wrestle with the problem of what a high-stakes test ought to measure.

You see, once a state legislature formally enacted a law establishing a statewide minimum competency testing program, the law's implementation was usually turned over to that state's education department. And when officials of the education department moved forward to create the authorized assessment program, those officials

5

typically entered into a contract with an external test development firm to carry out the test's construction. It was true then and it's still true now: Few state departments of education possess the in-house capacity to generate high-stakes assessments—meaning most must rely on substantial external assistance.

Having chosen a test development contractor (for example, CTB-McGraw-Hill of Monterey, California), the next step for state officials was to determine the nature of the skills and knowledge to be measured. Ordinarily, these decisions were made by a committee of that state's educators. For example, if the state's competency testing legislation called for a test in reading, a test in mathematics, and a test in written composition, state authorities would typically appoint a committee of 20–30 teachers and curriculum specialists for each of the three subject areas. These committees, usually operating under the guidance of the external contractor's staff, would identify which skills and knowledge in each subject area their state's upcoming competency test would measure.

With few exceptions, these committees of educators selected remarkably low-level sets of basic skills and knowledge. Indeed, a more appropriate label for these early minimum competency tests would have been *"most minimum imaginable* competency tests." Let me explain why.

To do so properly, however, I need to take another brief dip into my own experiences. I used to be a test developer. In 1968, I formed a small nonprofit organization, called the Instructional Objectives Exchange (IOX), to create behaviorally stated instructional objectives and distribute them to U.S. educators. I abhor wheel reinvention, and during this period it struck me that too many of the nation's educators were cranking out redundant behavioral objectives. I thought a national clearinghouse for such objectives would help.

Later, in the mid-1970s, we set up a successor organization, known as IOX Assessment Associates, with the purpose of developing high-stakes tests for state departments of education and for large school districts. I soon began to realize that the important tests we were creating would significantly influence what teachers actually taught. As a result of this insight, I found my own career interests turning from instruction and heading toward educational measurement. I soon became so enamored of assessment that, after doing a ton of assessment-related reading, I began teaching UCLA's graduate classes in educational measurement.

When IOX entered the test development arena, I was hoping to create high-stakes tests that would clarify assessment targets and help teachers to design on-target, more effective lessons. Testing, as I saw it, could be a potent force for instructional improvement *if* the tests were deliberately built with that mission in mind.

For more than a decade IOX served as the external test development contractor for a dozen states and several large school districts. During this period, I sat in on many state curriculum committee meetings convened to decide what sorts of skills and bodies of knowledge the state-legislated competency test would assess. You might as well learn what happened during those deliberations: The chief reason that most states ended up with *minimum* competency tests is that the committees of educators who chose the content to be tested invariably decided to assess truly low-level content.

Because I personally moderated many of these meetings and watched dozens of content-determining sessions take place, I can report that the majority of committee members didn't want to establish genuinely high-level expectations for the competency tests. They realized that denying diplomas or grade promotions to many students because of low test scores would reflect unfavorably on *teachers*. So, more often than not, the subject matter committees simply surrendered to the selection of low-level skills and knowledge. The result: competency tests that measured minima.

Once a minimum competency test was in place, the teachers who were chiefly responsible for teaching students to master its content (usually English teachers and mathematics teachers) devoted considerable energy to having their students pass the tests. Teachers did not wish to face the disgruntled parents of students who had failed the tests, even if what many high school graduation tests actually measured was sometimes barely more sophisticated than material 6th grade students ought to have learned.

Not surprisingly, thanks to the low level of the assessment

targets, relatively few students ultimately failed to pass these early-vintage minimum competency tests. Failing students were typically given opportunities to re-take the test and achieve a passing score. But even so, in most schools, at least *some* students failed—and thus were denied diplomas.

It didn't take the press long to figure out that something potentially newsworthy was taking place. Newspapers could easily write stories that compared schools within a district on the basis of competency test failure rates (and subsequent diploma denial). Consequently, a public perception began to emerge that schools in which few students failed were good schools, and schools in which many students failed were bad schools. The quality of schooling was being linked to the quality of students' test scores. And, as we shall see, once this approach to judging schools took root, it flourished.

The Elementary and Secondary Education Act (ESEA) of 1965

Another factor nurtured the notion that a school's quality could be determined by its students' test scores, and that factor was an important piece of federal legislation. The Elementary and Secondary Education Act (ESEA) of 1965 was the first major federal law dispensing significant amounts of money to U.S. school districts for the support of locally designed programs intended to bolster children's learning. Prior to the 1965 enactment of ESEA, the amount of federal dollars flowing from Washington, D.C., to local schools had been relatively modest. ESEA, by contrast, promised truly big bucks for local educators.

The newness of ESEA's federal funds-for-education strategy led Congress to build in a number of corresponding safeguards. One of the most influential was championed by Robert Kennedy, then a senator from New York. Kennedy's addition to the law required educators receiving ESEA dollars to demonstrate that these funds were being well spent—namely, by evaluating and reporting on the effectiveness of their federally supported programs. According to the new law, if local officials did not formally evaluate the current year's federally subsidized program, then they would not receive

8

next year's ESEA funds. In truth, it was not all that important whether a program's evaluation was positive or negative, at least in the early days of ESEA funding. Just *conducting* the evaluation was all that was necessary.

Given the potency of the "green carrot," it should come as no shock that educators who were getting ESEA awards scurried madly about in an effort to document the success of their ESEA-funded programs. And because almost all these programs were aimed directly at improving students' basic skills, the first step for most local educators was to identify suitable tests that could determine whether students were in fact learning the three Rs. The most readily available tests were off-the-shelf, standardized achievement tests such as the Metropolitan Achievement Tests or the Comprehensive Tests of Basic Skills. These sorts of tests became almost everyone's choice to evaluate whether ESEA-supported programs were working, because they (1) had been developed by respected measurement companies, (2) were widely available, and (3) were regarded as technically first-rate.

Then, as now, few educators knew much about test development and were generally willing to leave the creation of tests to the specialists. As a result, most of the educators whose work depended on ESEA dollars readily accepted that students' scores on these celebrated off-the-shelf, standardized achievement tests accurately determined the quality of classroom instruction. The unfortunate truth was that what these standardized tests were measuring often had only a faint relationship to the skills and knowledge being promoted by a particular ESEA-funded program. Sadly, few members of the education profession cried foul, and the use of standardized achievement test scores to determine an ESEA program's success became the national norm.

Both policymakers and the general body of educators made what must have seemed the logical next step in assessment application: If standardized achievement tests could ascertain the effectiveness of ESEA-funded, basic skills-focused instructional programs, they could be employed to evaluate the success of other types of instructional programs as well. Having bought into the idea that certain kinds of instructional quality could be determined by using standardized achievement tests, policymakers were pretty well locked into the position that those tests did in fact provide defensible estimates of instructional quality.

Although ESEA of 1965 certainly stimulated a vastly increased reliance on standardized achievement tests as a way of judging educational success, U.S. educators must accept the blame for simply rolling over and allowing their teaching to be evaluated by students' scores on those off-the-shelf tests. As you'll read in later chapters, that wrong-headed acquiescence has led to a series of educational practices that have seriously eroded the quality of today's schooling.

Newspapers Take Notice

By the late 1980s, most states had established some kind of mandatory statewide testing program. Although many of these assessment programs consisted of the sorts of low-level competency tests I've already described, some state authorities, troubled by their competency tests' low expectations, had set about to renovate their initial minimum competency testing programs to assess more demanding outcomes. Some states preferred to revise their own competency tests (typically with a contractor's help). Other states simply selected one of the nationally published standardized achievement tests. Thus, usually in the spring, a statewide test was administered to all students in selected grades (for instance, in grades 3, 5, 8, and 11). The most ambitious states chose to administer achievement tests to students in *every* grade, usually starting with grade 3.

Tests scores were sent to local districts and schools so that educators and parents could see how students had performed. At that time, test results were *not* routinely sent to newspapers. Indeed, for the most part, local newspapers displayed little interest in these test results.

And then came the day (rumored by some to have been a "slow news day") that the first newspaper reporter obtained a copy of statewide test results and wrote a story that used students' test scores to *rank* districts and schools within the state. This ranking system allowed parents to quickly see how their child's school stacked up against other schools. And because most educators had previously accepted the idea that scores on standardized achievement tests indicated the effectiveness of educational programs, the press soon billed these annual rankings as reflections of educational quality. Highly ranked schools were regarded as effective; lowly ranked schools were regarded as ineffective.

For a number of years now, I've been following these newspaper rankings in many localities, where they often attract as much attention as the publication of the winning numbers in the state lottery. These rankings invariably lead to judgments about which educators are doing good jobs and which are doing bad jobs. And because citizens believe that high scores signify successful instruction, the annual rankings place enormous pressure on teachers to improve their students' scores on statewide tests.

Some of these statewide tests are off-the-shelf, national standardized achievement tests, some are customized tests built exclusively for a particular state, and some are a combination of national and customized items. All these tests, however, are standardized in the sense that they are administered and scored in a uniform, predetermined manner. Incidentally, most citizens tend to ascribe more credibility to national achievement tests, five of which are currently used in our public schools: California Achievement Tests, Comprehensive Tests of Basic Skills, Iowa Tests of Basic Skills, Metropolitan Achievement Tests, and Stanford Achievement Tests. In general, folks place less trust in customized, state-specific standardized tests, regarding these "home grown" tests as more likely to have been softened to make the state's educators look good.

But customized or national, when newspapers run their annual rankings of district-by-district and school-by-school scores, there is a clear message to all concerned: *These rankings reflect instructional quality.* Given that message, I am surprised that newspaper editors do not publish these score-based school rankings in their sports sections, along with team standings in basketball, baseball, and football. Americans love contests—and while we derive modest gratification from applauding a winner, we appear to get more fundamental joy from identifying losers. Yes, the sports pages are the natural home for score-based school rankings.

Scoreboard-Induced Motivation

As we all know, the 1990s brought a tremendous increase in the reliance on students' standardized achievement test scores as indicators of instructional quality. Think about the name of the tests for a moment: *achievement* tests. Because an achievement test would seem to measure what students achieve—that is, what they learn in school—it's natural to perceive it as a suitable measure of what kids have been taught in school. As you'll read in Chapters 3 and 4, that perception is plumb wrong.

The attention given to achievement test scores and the tacit implication that students' test scores provide an accurate index of educational success helped fuel an enormous preoccupation with those scores during the last decade. School boards demanded that their district's educators improve students' test performances. School administrators at all levels were evaluated almost exclusively on the basis of students' scores on standardized achievement tests. And more than a few governors pinned their political aspirations directly to the elevation of their state's test scores. California Governor Gray Davis, for example, made the improvement of test scores so central to his administration's success that he publicly proclaimed he would forgo any bid to seek the U.S. presidency if his state's scores failed to rise. George W. Bush made Texas's rising test scores a central element in his successful presidential campaign.

Now, in 2001, there's no question that a score-boosting sweepstakes has enveloped the nation. Who has been tasked with boosting students' test scores? Teachers and administrators, of course. And it is precisely because teachers and administrators are under such pressure these days to bring about improvements in students' test scores that I have written this book.

U.S. educators have been thrown into a score-boosting game they cannot win. More accurately, the score-boosting game cannot be won without doing educational damage to the children in our public schools. The negative consequences flowing from a national enshrinement of increased test scores are both widespread and serious. Chapter 1 highlights the most harmful of these consequences.

But let's get one thing straight: I do not believe America's educators are the guiltless victims of an evil imposed by wrong-thinking policymakers. I think the education profession itself is fundamentally at fault. We allowed students' test scores to become the indicator of our effectiveness. We failed to halt the profound misuse of standardized achievement tests to judge our educational quality. We let this happen to ourselves. And more grievously, we let it happen to the children we are supposed to be educating. Shame on us.

It's not too late to alter this sorry state of affairs. As the book proceeds, I'll describe a strategy for modifying what has become an untenable measurement context for appraising the nation's schools. I hope you, and other readers, will take seriously my challenge to change this situation.

Classroom Consequences of Unsound High-Stakes Testing

I AM NOT OPPOSED TO EDUCATIONAL TESTING. IF PROPERLY BUILT AND SENSIbly used, educational tests can help teachers deliver effective instruction. I am not even opposed to high-stakes testing, if the tests being used are *suitable*. That "if" clause, of course, is a significant one. The current high-stakes testing programs I'm familiar with are definitely *not* suitable.

Let me put it another way. The most serious consideration in the generation and use of a high-stakes testing program is whether the tests being employed actually help or hinder the quality of the education children receive. I believe it is possible to put together a statewide high-stakes testing program that can simultaneously supply evidence about the quality of the state's schools *and* help teachers promote students' mastery of truly worthwhile skills and knowledge. The trick, of course, is to employ educational tests that can fulfill an accountability function while also supplying teachers with suitable instructional targets. If an assessment program incorporates the right kinds of high-stakes tests, it can make significant contributions to children's educations. Given the wretched quality of today's high-stakes tests, however, their effects on students are more bad than good.

As you read this chapter, I need you to at least temporarily accept my assertion that the vast majority of today's high-stakes tests are bad—that is, their use hurts the quality of children's schooling. I promise to demonstrate in Chapters 3 and 4 why the assumption you have kindly accepted coincides with reality.

Misdirected Pressures on Educators

As I indicated in the Introduction, today's educators are increasingly caught up in a measurement-induced maelstrom focused on raising students' scores on high-stakes tests. The term "maelstrom" captures all too accurately the reality of this test-obsession: It's a hazardous whirlpool that can drag us down, even when we approach it cautiously.

Because U.S. society currently accepts the idea that good test scores equal good education, everybody wants students to score well on high-stakes tests. The first negative effect of today's high-stakes testing programs is that such programs divert educators' attention from the genuinely important educational decisions they ought to be making. Thousands of American educators find themselves caught up in a score-boosting obsession that seriously detracts from their effectiveness in teaching children. The critical question of "How do we teach Tracy the things she needs to know?" is forced aside by this far less important one: "How do we improve Tracy's scores on the high-stakes test she will be taking?"

As I suggested earlier, there is no intrinsic reason why high-stakes testing programs can't contribute to improving Tracy's education. But for that to happen, we must employ the right kind of high-stakes tests. And the tests now being used in high-stakes assessment programs are generally all wrong.

The most frightening aspect of the pressure on educators to raise test scores is that it's a score-boosting game that educators have no chance to win—at least, not without harming children. I'll clarify this point in Chapters 3 and 4 and show you why today's high-stakes tests preclude any legitimate way for educators to succeed.

Misidentification of Inferior and Superior Schools

As soon as score-based rankings of schools commenced in the United States, it was natural for people to believe that schools with high-scoring students were successful and schools with low-scoring students were the opposite. For several years, these high-to-low rankings were the only information about "school quality" available to the public; no one thought to collect any other kind of evidence. Parents recognized whether their child's school was ranked high or ranked low, and those rankings usually made at least some difference to educators and had some influence on the way teachers taught.

But then came the 1990s, when public and political cries for accountability focused efforts to raise test scores on the schools with the lowest rankings—where score boosts were most likely to be achieved. After all, on statistical grounds alone, it is easier to elevate the performance of low-scoring students than it is to elevate the scores of any other groups of students. It's also politically attractive for policymakers to reach out in an effort to "rescue" low-performing students.

Today, this practice of singling out low-scoring schools to urge their instructional staffs to shape up "unacceptable" performances is incredibly widespread. Sometimes it's done by publicly identifying low-scoring schools as weak (with the hope that such a characterization will spur the school's staff to do a better job). In other instances, district or state officials provide low-performing schools with additional support services, such as increased supervision or more staff-development funds. Several states have adopted policies that call for "grading" individual schools on the basis of students' high-stakes test scores. As one example, students enrolled in a Florida school receiving consecutive failing grades were to be given vouchers so they could use state funds to obtain education elsewhere, even in private schools.

In almost all instances involving the use of test scores to evaluate the quality of schooling, low-performing schools receive a *label*. Some of these labels are fairly neutral, such as "low-performing school." Others are genuinely denigrating, such as "failing school." But whether the labels are bland or bleak, you can be sure of one thing: The staff members at a negatively labeled school are certain to feel awful about the way they have been identified.

The really troubling element of labeling schools as "inferior" is that in many instances those labels are just plain wrong. The staff of a "failing" school may actually have been doing a superlative in-structional job, but their efforts did not get reflected by students' scores on the *wrong* high-stakes achievement test. (Don't forget your chapter-long assumption.)

Equally bad, in my view, is the practice of identifying schools—and teachers—as successful simply because their students score well on standardized achievement tests. As you'll soon read, a meaningful amount of what's measured by today's high-stakes tests is directly attributable not to what students learn in school, but to what they *bring* to school in the form of their families' socioeco-nomic status or the academic aptitudes they happened to inherit. If a school has a student body drawn largely from affluent homes, you can be almost certain that its students' will put up lofty numbers on high-stakes tests. But this doesn't render that school's staff effective. In fact, there is often some genuinely abysmal instruction taking place in the wealthiest schools. Yet because of students' high scores on the *wrong* tests, the staff is thought to be doing a superb job. Whether students attend affluent schools or poverty-level schools, they *all* need the best instruction we can provide. Today's high-stakes tests often mask the actual quality of instruction in schools serving both low-income and high-income families.

Naturally, the massive misidentification of schools' effectiveness leads to all sorts of instructional folly. Skillful teachers in "failing" schools are told to change their instructional techniques—tech-niques that, by any accurate evaluation, would be regarded as suc-cessful. Weak teachers in schools with high-scoring students tend to rest on their unwarranted instructional laurels when, in fact, they should be significantly altering how they teach. And, as I'll point out in a moment, we're seeing a rising level of educationally reprehensible activities within the classrooms of schools that have been labeled "inferior."

The adverse effects of school-quality misidentification don't stop with teachers. Students, too, are harmed by inaccurate judgments about the quality of their schools—especially students who attend a "failing" school. As I suggested previously, most schools misidentified as inferior will likely be located in disadvantaged settings. Children who grow up in these environments often have fewer positive experiences than children who grow up in more advantaged settings. As a consequence, disadvantaged youngsters frequently don't feel all that marvelous about themselves or about what life has dished out to them. Now add to that mixture the harsh judgment, "You go to a bad school." It's one more slap at these children—and all the more objectionable because the quality of the school has not been accurately evaluated. And that incorrect evaluation occurs because the *wrong* high-stakes test has been used.

Curricular Reductionism

Because today's educators are under such intense pressure to raise their students' scores on high-stakes tests, we are witnessing a nationwide diminishment of curricular attention toward any subject that isn't included on a high-stakes test. As many beleaguered educators will comment, "If our chief job is to raise test scores, why waste time teaching content that's not even tested?" This curricular exodus is seen in almost any setting where high-stakes tests dominate.

Let's not sneer too quickly at teachers who fail to teach what isn't tested. This is an altogether human response to a reward structure that focuses exclusively on a single criterion (whether that criterion is well founded or not). If people find themselves in a context where the rewards come from X, and there are no rewards for Y, which do you think will typically be promoted? Teachers are no more or less susceptible to such reward/punishment structures than anyone else.

And remember, the pressure to raise scores on high-stakes tests can be *enormous*. Many educational policymakers, such as members of school boards and highly placed educational administrators, truly believe that improved scores on a high-stakes test—any high-stakes test—equal improved education. If they really believe this, then it is not surprising that they will attempt to assert every possible pressure on educators to boost students' test scores. A teacher who is constantly pummeled with score-boosting messages soon learns this lesson: *Teach what is tested; avoid what isn't.*

In such a milieu, the first content areas to go are the "frill" subjects, such as music and art. In many elementary schools where pursuit of high-stakes testing predominates, it is nearly impossible to see a trace of art or hear a note of music. From a test-focused teacher's perspective, any time spent on these two "fringe subjects" will cut into time that could be devoted to what's measured by the high-stakes test. There's no time for cartoons or tunes in a test-prep factory.

But the content-pruning knife cuts deeper. If a statewide high-stakes test focuses only on language arts and mathematics, then watch how quickly teachers' curricular attention shifts away from social studies and science. Children may be learning about "survival of the fittest" in science class, but their teachers are subscribing to this quasi-Darwinian curricular dictum: "Survival of *content* that *fittest best* the high-stakes test."

And the intellectual fabric of what's taught—even within the tested subject areas—also tends to be dramatically distorted. For example, if the high-stakes test in mathematics deals only with low-level cognitive challenges, you can be pretty sure that few classrooms will push students' higher-level mathematical skills. If lower-level language arts content is assessed, then lower-level language arts content will be taught. Thus, what's assessed in a high-stakes testing program not only restricts the curricular content areas, it restricts the nature of the cognitive operations students face in the content areas that *are* assessed.

In sum, the curricular content assessed by high-stakes tests tends to drive other subjects and other cognitive skills from teachers' classrooms. The erosion of a rich curriculum clearly robs our children of important things they should be learning. For them, the ultimate consequence of unsound high-states testing is a seriously diminished education.

I am not castigating *all* educators for committing the kinds of curricular sins I've just described. There are many who have not succumbed to test-induced curricular reduction pressures. Nor for that matter am I blaming individual teachers for behaving in a way that the explosion of high-stakes testing pressures literally forces them to behave. Teachers are not the villains in this assessment saga; they are more like victims. Unfortunately, the ultimate victims are the students.

The perpetrators of this assessment-spawned debacle are the individuals, well intentioned for the most part, who establish and support high-stakes testing that does educational harm. We must alter the policies that allow such misguided assessment programs to flourish. I'll suggest how to do that later in the book.

Drill and Kill

Closely related to curricular reductionism is the tendency of numerous test-oppressed teachers to drill their students relentlessly on the types of test items contained in the particular high-stakes test their students must pass. My closet is crammed with all sorts of test-focused materials that commercial vendors have cranked out in the last five years to "help raise your students' test scores." These test preparation materials, clearly intended to make a profit from test-oppressed school systems, are mostly an endless array of practice exercises—and the closer the practice items are to the items on the "real" high-stakes test, the better.

But incessant "skill and drill" often turns into "drill and kill"—that is, such repetitive instructional activities tend to deaden students' genuine interest in learning. All the excitement and intellectual vibrancy that students might encounter during a really interesting lesson are driven out by a tedious, test-fostered series of drills. In fact, one fairly certain way of telling whether a high-stakes test is a winner or loser is to see if unexciting drill activities can actually *raise* students' test scores. If so, the test is almost certainly inappropriate—measuring only low-level outcomes.

Yes, test-spawned, skill-and-drill instruction can indeed help students develop low-level cognitive skills and teach them to recite memorized information, but at what cost? Teachers who are so driven to raise test scores that they transform their classrooms into cram-focused, assembly-line factories risk extinguishing their students' love of learning. And they may even be chasing some students out of school, particularly those students whom our society most needs to have a decent education. I've spoken with a number of teachers who admitted that pressures to boost test scores in their district are leading to a drill-focused form of schooling that inclines both disadvantaged students and second-language students to want to give up on school. If learning is no fun, and if all teachers do is drill, it's not surprising that some students seek a permanent recess.

Test-Pressured Cheating

Perhaps the most reprehensible of the acts test-pressured teachers engage in can be summed up in a single word: *cheating*. Historically, it's been the teachers who have had to be alert for student cheating; today, more and more of those caught cheating on tests are the teachers themselves.

Educator-initiated cheating is not totally new, of course. Twenty years ago, I delivered a scheduled speech in a school district where, one day earlier, the district's administrators had been accused in the local newspaper of modifying 1,800 student answer sheets—substituting correct responses for incorrect ones. After I dutifully concluded my remarks, the bulk of the question period focused not on the content of my speech (which, as I recall, was fairly dazzling), but on the cheating scandal and the district superintendent's role in that escapade.

This kind of incident was rare enough in its time for me to remember it clearly all these years later. Educator-initiated cheating is much more common today, unquestionably stimulated by the score-raising pressure of high-stakes assessment programs. During the 1999–2000 academic year, for example, 52 educators from the New York City public schools were charged with test-related cheating. In June 2001, the principal of a highly-ranked Maryland elementary school resigned after allegations that 5th grade students taking the annual, high-stakes state achievement test were guided toward correct answers and given help rewriting essay responses. Similar reports about outright violations of state- or district-prescribed test administration procedures appear almost every week. Teachers and administrators caught engaging in such rule bending have sometimes lost their teaching certificates and, in many instances, have actually lost their jobs.

In recent years, two general categories of educators' test-pressured cheating have come to light. One is obvious and embarrassing. The other is subtle and insidious. At the most obvious level, we find the blatant rule breaking. These are the teachers and administrators who, during the administration of a high-stakes test, (1) give their students more than the stipulated time to complete the test, (2) dispense hints about what a given item's correct answer ought to be, or (3) review finished tests and urge students to "rethink and revise" their responses.

I even recall a case in which students were directed to write their test answers on scratch paper. Only after the teachers checked these answers and suggested modifications were students allowed to transfer their "improved" answers to the test's actual response sheet. This process has the added benefit of reducing the number of erasures on the students' formal response sheet. Teachers have learned that an answer sheet with excessive erasures is more likely to be identified by test-scoring personnel as needing more careful scrutiny. And teachers engaged in a score-boosting conspiracy do not want their students' response sheets to get any extra scrutiny.

But the sort of teacher-initiated, test-pressured cheating I find the most reprehensible is what can be called *instructionally corrupt test preparation*. This occurs when teachers either design their instruction around actual items taken from a high-stakes test or teach toward *clone items*—items only slightly different from the test's actual items. Teachers, you see, typically have access to a test's items before those items are administered, and are sure to see this year's test before the test is administered again next year. With copying machines so readily available these days, it is almost impossible to stop teachers from "familiarizing" themselves with a high-stakes test's actual items.

One widely used standardized achievement test begins each level of its reading tests by presenting 16 specific words for which students must identify appropriate synonyms. If you are a test-pressured teacher who administers this test in the spring, don't you make sure that next year's students will encounter most of those 16 words before next year's test? Teachers may be oppressed, but they're not stupid.

Let's be blunt: This instructionally corrupt test preparation is a very effective way of raising students' scores on a high-stakes test. After all, the students have received teacher-guided practice in answering the test's actual items (or mirror images of those items). Although children's test scores may improve, their mastery of the content on which the test is based may remain unchanged. What emerges from testing is an altogether inaccurate picture of a student's true level of achievement. In turn, these inaccurate performance level assessments lead teachers to make inappropriate instructional decisions about those students.

Bad Things in Bundles

To sum up, some terrible things are happening in U.S. public schools—and they're happening as a direct consequence of ill-conceived high-stakes testing programs. Even worse, these bad things are happening with increasing frequency and seriousness. Although the architects of high-stakes assessment programs are genuinely well intentioned, their efforts have harmed children rather than helped them.

And the nation's educators are every bit as guilty. After all, we allowed our instructional effectiveness to be determined by students' scores on tests that were never built to be determiners of school success. We sat back meekly as newspapers publicly equated test scores with our instructional skill.

The kinds of test-induced evils I describe in this chapter are increasingly prevalent because we let them happen. Most regrettably, we let them happen to our students. Let me be clear about one thing: I am every bit as guilty as the next bloke because, until recently, I didn't realize how widespread these test-induced problems really are. I didn't realize how truly awful are the effects on children. I should have been speaking out years ago and writing up a storm to dissuade people from doing dumb things with high-stakes tests. My culpability, you can be sure, matches yours.

During the last three years, I've been trying to make up for my sins of omission. Having been raised in a religious home, I understand the payoffs of doing one's penance. But I need help from other educators who are also in a penance-paying mood. We must take action to halt the harm that unsound high-stakes assessment programs are doing to our children. As you continue reading this book, I hope you'll be moved to undertake one or more of the fix-it suggestions and action options I'll be offering.

Why We Test

ONE OF THE CHIEF REASONS THAT EDUCATORS PASSIVELY SUFFER THE IN-creasingly serious set of test-induced difficulties in their classrooms is that, by and large, the educational community is woefully ignorant about measurement. This *assessment illiteracy* has induced many of us to watch, not act, as unsound high-stakes testing programs—and the unsound tests featured in those programs—continue their insidious spread.

Consequences of Assessment Illiteracy

I don't mean that U.S. teachers and educational administrators are totally ignorant about testing. During our own student days, we were on the receiving end of tests galore. As teachers, we have churned out our share of classroom quizzes, exams, and tests. All educators know *something* about assessment.

But if educators were to be completely candid, most of us would probably admit that our understanding of educational measurement doesn't extend much beyond the care and feeding of teacher-made classroom tests. By and large, we think of educational measurement as a quantitative technical specialty that, while perhaps not as complex as rocket science, is well beyond our comfort zone, if not our comprehension.

That's just what I thought when I was in graduate school. In fact, I was so caught up in learning about curriculum and instruction that my doctoral studies didn't include a single course in educational measurement. Everything I now know about assessment has come either from books or from my own experience trying to build tests that might help teachers teach better.

I believe that it's largely because so few educators have received training in educational measurement that so many of us continue to perceive assessment as intimidating. The majority of U.S. states do not require prospective teachers or administrators to complete a single course in educational measurement. And even though some educators have taken a course in measurement, chances are that the course was taught according to a fairly traditional conception of the subject—one that is far removed from the realities of assessment in today's classrooms. Educators unfamiliar with measurement have allowed all sorts of assessment-rooted policies to be imposed on them. This acquiescence, as we have seen, has permitted assessment programs to have a decidedly negative effect on teaching and learning. One of my first pleas to educators is quite straightforward: Please become at least reasonably assessment literate.

If you set out to learn what you really need to know about educational testing, you'll soon discover that it's not a mysterious, esoteric field. To be sure, there are some fairly quantitative processes associated with contemporary testing programs. But what most educators *need to know* about testing is quite straightforward, and not very quantitative at all. If you sit down for an evening or two with any good introductory measurement text (see the References and Resources section at the end of this book for some recommendations), you'll be able to learn what you truly must know to stop the misuse of high-stakes tests. In fact, you will pick up a few of today's required assessment concepts before you've finished this book. In that vein, let's start right now by examining a couple of important notions linked to why educators test students at all.

An Inference-Making Enterprise

Educational testing revolves around inferences. Typically, we test a child to infer what the child knows or can do. We can also assess children to get a fix on their attitudes or their interests. Teachers need this kind of information to make sensible instructional decisions about their students. If Tamara has already mastered an important mathematical skill, and Tamara's teacher can determine this by having Tamara take a quiz, then the teacher can move on to other mathematical content for Tamara. If Clyde shows on a classroom test that he knows his multiplication tables through the number nine, then Clyde's teacher need not teach him about the mysteries of six times seven. That's the chief mission of classroom tests: to capture the kind of information teachers need so they can make better instructional decisions.

But there's a ton of stuff to teach children, and only so much time to teach it. If teachers tried to test students on *everything* the students might have learned, there would be precious little time left over for instructional activities. Moreover, requiring students to spend three or four hours per day completing a seemingly interminable array of tests seems like a sure way to incite them to revolution.

To avoid such ugly consequences, teachers build tests to *sample* a student's knowledge and skills, and they choose test items to represent larger bodies of knowledge or skill. Based on a student's performance on the test's sample, the teacher makes an inference about the student's knowledge and skills. In Figure 2.1, I've illustrated the ideal relationship of *content, assessment, inferences*, and *decisions* within the instructional process. By "content" I mean the combination of knowledge and skills—and sometimes the affective outcomes—that are the object of a teacher's instruction. The assessment samples the larger body of content. Based on students' responses to the assessment, the teacher infers the degree to which the student has mastered that larger body of content. Finally, relying on such inferences, the teacher decides how best to teach the students.

2.1 **Assessment's Ideal Role Within the Instructional Process**

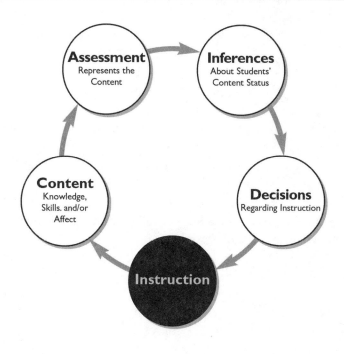

Putting it another way, students' overt performances on sample-based tests help teachers arrive at inferences about the students' covert knowledge and skills. It's fairly obvious that you can't tell whether a student can write a persuasive essay merely by looking at the student. But if your final exam asks the student to write a pair of persuasive essays, and the student performs well on both essays, you can reasonably infer that the student is a capable writer of persuasive essays.

Most educators hear the expression "a valid test" hundreds of times throughout their careers. Well, technically, it is not the test that's valid or invalid; rather, it is the *inference* made about a student, based on the student's test performance. If Charley scores well on a vocabulary quiz, the teacher infers that Charley has mastered most or all of the vocabulary terms that the test sampled. Clearly, the more satisfactorily a test represents the body of knowledge, skills, and affect it is supposed to represent, the more valid will be any inference about a student's status with respect to what's been measured. But "satisfactoriness" of representation is influenced heavily by the size of a test's sample. The trick is to create a satisfactory representation in the real-world time available for testing.

Although a test may be described as *reliable* or *unreliable*, because reliability focuses on the consistency with which the test does its measurement job, it can never be *valid* or *invalid*. Again, it's the score-based inferences that we make about a student or a group of students that are valid or invalid.

In the previous chapter, I described teachers who relentlessly drill students on actual items lifted from an existing high-stakes test. Can you see how such test-preparation activities completely negate the validity of any score-based inference about what a student knows? The student's score on the high-stakes test sample might soar because of the student's total familiarity with those particular items. Yet, if you were to give the student a test containing different items measuring the identical cognitive skill, the student's apparent mastery would evaporate.

Teachers who teach toward actual test items, or toward clones of those items, are almost certain to destroy the validity of any score-based inferences about students' levels of mastery. Children who need instructional help won't get it, because their test performances make it appear that they know what's being tested—but, of course, they don't. In reality, all they know is how to respond to a particular set of test items: those in the sample. Validity vanishes. This loss of assessment validity is epidemic across the United States because of the validity-eroding activities fostered by flawed high-stakes testing programs.

In the same way that teachers are responsible for making valid inferences about students based on classroom test scores, the policymakers behind high-stakes testing programs also need to draw valid inferences from students' scores on high-stakes tests. Actually, high-stakes testing programs should yield two levels of inference. First, there's the score-based inference about a student's current knowledge or skills. We use an individual student's score to infer the student's level of mastery. Typically, students' high-stakes test scores are aggregated so that, for example, we can compare the average test score at each school, and then rank the schools from highest average score to lowest average score. This leads to the second-level inference, which is related to what students' test scores reveal about the schools they attend. The typical second-level inference is that high-scoring schools are instructionally good and low-scoring schools are instructionally bad.

Both first-level and second-level inferences about students' scores on high-stakes tests can be valid or invalid. As you'll see in the next two chapters, in most current high-stakes testing programs, both the first-level and the second-level inferences are not only mildly invalid—they are rocko-socko, *unquestionably* invalid!

I often hear technical measurement constructs such as "validity" and "reliability" tossed around flippantly these days by folks who wouldn't recognize an unreliable test if it chewed on their leg. And validity! The validity of score-based inferences is eminently contestable. People often make invalid inferences about the meaning of a child's score on a standardized achievement test. They also frequently make invalid inferences about the quality of a school's teaching staff, based on students' aggregated scores on such tests. Let me say it again: *Test-based inferences can be valid or invalid.* And educators have, for the most part, been much too meek in accepting as valid the inferences made by measurement specialists.

While I'm banging on this particular drum, I want to rant for a moment or two more about a quality mistakenly attributed to most high-stakes educational tests. Typically, these tests yield numbers . . . and some of these numbers even contain a decimal point! And because such tests almost always comprise items devised by high-powered national testing firms, many educators believe that there is great precision in the resultant test scores. Don't you believe it. A child can take a national standardized achievement test on Monday, retake the same test on Tuesday, and come up with significantly different scores each time. Kids feel different on different days. Things happen in their lives to produce such differences. Distractions can occur right before a high-stakes test is taken—or during the test-taking session itself. Scores can change.

I don't wish to suggest that scores on well-constructed tests are meaningless. Of course they aren't. But they aren't so accurate that educators need to genuflect to the precision of any given score. Scores on important, properly constructed tests give us a reasonably accurate fix on a youngster—but not to two digits beyond the decimal point.

Thus, a school's average year-to-year increase of a point or two on a high-stakes test should hardly be a springboard for jubilation. Odds are that it's just a chance-based increase. Likewise, score-drops of a few points can be caused by all sorts of trivial events. The standardized tests used in education simply aren't as super-accurate as most folks think.

Multiple Measurement Missions

Classroom tests, the kinds teachers construct, are almost always used for one of three purposes: (1) to give students grades, (2) to motivate students, or (3) to help make instructional decisions. When I was a high school teacher, using tests to make instructional decisions never even entered my consciousness. Along with most of my fellow teachers, I used tests for one purpose only: to assign grades. Even today, the majority of teachers employ tests either for grade-dispensation ("If you scored higher than 95 percent on the midterm exam, you will get a grade of *A*.") or for motivation ("Study hard, students, because the final exam is right around the corner!").

Increasingly, however, teachers are beginning to use the results of classroom assessments to help them decide how to teach their students. More teachers now recognize that test-derived inferences about students' status (with respect, for example, to an instructional objective being promoted) can help determine whether to provide additional instruction on a particular topic or, instead, move on to a new topic. This embrace of testing's instructional implications is a tremendously positive development—and one that educators must continue to encourage.

A lot of today's teachers also realize that by using some variation of a pretest/post-test data-gathering model, they can get an idea of how well they've taught. If students' pretest performance is putrid, but their post-test performance is polished, then a teacher ought to be satisfied with those results. On the other hand, if students' post-test performances are decisively worse than their pretest efforts, then a teacher should begin wondering about the quality of the "instruction" provided between the two tests. (In Chapter 7, I'll describe a way to collect pretest and post-test evidence that can supply a pretty accurate picture of a teacher's instructional success.)

Classroom assessments, then, are usually focused chiefly on grading students and informing the teacher's instructional decisions. What are the main objectives of *large-scale assessments?* By large-scale assessments, I mean the kinds of statewide testing programs or district-level testing programs that may or may not constitute a high-stakes testing operation. Let's pause for a moment to consider the two main conditions that must exist before a large-scale assessment program can be considered a high-stakes testing program:

1. *There are significant consequences linked to individual students' test performance.* When the Chicago Public School system holds back students in the 8th grade because they didn't earn sufficiently high scores on the Iowa Tests of Basic Skills, it's clear that what's going on is a high-stakes testing program. It's high-stakes because the test results can make a meaningful difference to an individual student and to that student's family.

2. *The students' test scores determine the "instructional success" of a school or district.* Again, the usual inference is that higher-ranked schools are effective and lower-ranked schools are not. A growing number of states are linking serious consequences to large-scale assessments. In Florida, for example, schools whose students scored high on a state-developed achievement test were

assigned grades of *A*. Schools whose students scored badly got grades of *F*. If an *F*-graded school didn't improve, it soon found itself on the receiving end of a variety of state-stipulated penalties. States place all sorts of negative sanctions on low-scoring schools. Some sanctions go so far as to close these schools permanently. Other states now mandate financial rewards for high-scoring schools. In California, for example, sufficiently large gains in students' scores on the Stanford Achievement Tests could garner a $25,000 award for a school—or for an individual teacher.

But even if there are no tangible rewards or penalties linked to a school's score-based rank, those tests still qualify as high-stakes measurements. Almost everyone wants to succeed, and teachers want their school's students to score well. Few folks want to be at the bottom of what is seen to be a quality-ranking continuum. That's why there are few large-scale assessment programs these days that are not fundamentally high-stakes in nature. Even if state officials do not release score-based quality rankings, newspaper reporters—often relying on a state's freedom of information statutes—can almost always dig out the data needed to compile such rankings and create another widely read, attention-grabbing story about "school quality."

Having established that almost all large-scale assessment programs are high-stakes in nature, what is the primary measurement mission of such testing enterprises? The answer is an easy one, especially if you've actually been in our schools during the last few years. It's all about *accountability*.

Large-scale assessment programs, the bulk of which are of the high-stakes variety, are in place chiefly because someone believes that the annual collection of students' achievement scores will allow the public and educational policymakers (such as state school board members or state legislators) to see if educators are performing satisfactorily. Remember, most Americans believe that the quality of education is tied directly to students' test scores. They believe that by establishing a large-scale testing program that captures a student's score on an annual basis, they have created a mechanism that will allow all interested parties to monitor the caliber of schooling delivered.

If you look closely at the language of the typical state-level legislation establishing high-stakes assessment programs, you'll almost always find a statement expressing that in addition to its accountability function, the testing program is supposed to "make an instructional contribution." Don't be fooled by this. The reason that high-stakes testing programs were installed boils down to a single overriding mission: to create a measuring system that can be used to tell how well our children are being taught. In most instances, the instructional rhetoric is just that—*rhetoric.*

A Reasonable Motivation for Reformers

I currently subscribe to several assessment-related Internet list servers, in which many of the list's members express their belief that high-stakes testing represents a diabolical plot of the Left (or the Right) to discredit public schools (or privatize schooling, or possibly accomplish some other heinous goal). Perhaps those paranoid list-server people are correct, but I hope—and really believe—they are not. I continue to think that for the most part, those who establish high-stakes testing programs are well-intentioned folks.

I've spoken with a great many educational policymakers who simply want our schools to perform more successfully. And *if* their assumption that high student test scores reflect successful schooling were accurate, then creating assessment operations that allow policymakers to discern whether improvements are taking place would be very sensible thing to do. It would even make sense to think that schools ought to be ranked, from low to high, depending on how well a school's students score on these quality-indicating tests.

All this would be sensible, and our children would benefit, *if* the testing instruments used in large-scale assessment programs actually indicated how effectively a school's staff performed. Unfortunately, that's not what these tests do. And with that realization, the entire high-stakes assessment bubble bursts.

No, I don't think educational policymakers established high-stakes testing programs to harm children—or to "get" teachers. Nor do I think those policymakers acted out of malevolence. Rather, policymakers' actions reflect their ignorance of the reality of educational testing. Even worse, they don't know that they don't know.

From our positions within the educational community, we can see the truth that policymakers don't. U.S. educators must become more assessment literate so that we can make educational policymakers understand why the current high-stakes testing programs yield inaccurate pictures of educational quality. In the next two chapters, I'll explain why most existing high-stakes testing programs employ tests that do not provide accurate indications of educational effectiveness. The information in Chapters 3 and 4 must be thoroughly understood, because it needs to be relayed to the architects of today's high-stakes assessment programs. We need a collection of individual voices speaking in comprehensible language. I hope that you will personally take part in this important relay race.

The Mystique of
Standardized Measuring
Instruments

3

CERTAIN THINGS IN LIFE HAVE THE POWER TO INDUCE INSTANT DEFERENCE. Watch people's reactions when you look them squarely in the eye and utter any of the following phrases: "Internal Revenue Service," "lie detector test," or "subpoena." Those phrases refer to serious stuff—and stuff we take pretty seriously. Moreover, most of us defer to those who monitor whether taxes have been paid, lies told, or appearances made in court. At least some of this deference stems from our belief that the intricacies of federal tax accounting, polygraph truth detection, and what transpires in court are well beyond the normal person's comprehension. They may be right.

Toadying to Test People

In education, there's a similar sort of knee-jerk deference given to the folks who create and administer standardized tests. Whether the tests are (1) standardized *aptitude* tests, such as the ones that high school students take to get into college or (2) standardized *achievement* tests, such as the Iowa Tests of Basic Skills, most educators bow thoughtlessly to the purveyors of such tests. There are some exceptions, of course, but the vast majority of us believe that the technical innards of both lie detector tests and standardized tests are well beyond our ability to understand.

I realize that the people who develop and administer standardized tests possess some special skills, mostly quantitative in nature. Such folks are referred to by the somewhat intimidating title of *psychometrician*. But just remember that "psychometrician" is simply a ritzy (and self-anointed) synonym for a person who does testing. What I want you to realize from this chapter is that the essential truths about standardized measuring instruments are not terribly complicated.

I'm going to restrict my remarks to standardized *achievement* tests. Although I'll not be dealing with standardized *aptitude* tests, such as the SAT or the ACT (both college admissions exams), I don't want to suggest that these aptitude tests are beyond reproach. (Check out Nicholas Lemann's 1999 book *The Big Test* for an insightful analysis of the origins and problems with the SAT.) I've chosen to focus on achievement tests because these are the tests currently causing the most serious educational harm to our students.

I hope you'll read this chapter with sufficient care, so you'll be able to relay its chief points to at least one other person—preferably a nonfamily member. Within 48 hours of completing Chapter 3, I fully expect you to strong-arm some poor soul into hearing you recount the problems with standardized achievement tests.

The Objects of Our Attention

I have no personal quarrel with standardized achievement tests. As long as they're used appropriately, they can contribute important information to both teachers and parents. For instance, if we learn that Martina earned a relatively high score in language arts, but a relatively low score in science, we can make better instructional decisions about Martina. Nor am I a test-hater in general. As I mentioned in the previous chapter, I currently subscribe to Internet list servers in which many members appear eager to discard just about any kind of test other than the kind that teachers construct for their own classroom purposes. To most of these ardent test-be-gone critics, any form of standardized testing is repugnant. Well, I disagree. I think there are suitable roles for standardized achievement tests, but these roles do *not* include evaluating the instructional quality of (1) individual teachers or (2) the entire educational staff of a school.

Let me be more specific about the kinds of tests we're talking about. First off, as pointed out in the Introduction, a standardized test is any test that is administered and scored in a standard, predetermined manner. Currently, there are five widely used standardized achievement tests distributed throughout the United States: California Achievement Tests, Comprehensive Tests of Basic Skills, Iowa Tests of Basic Skills, Metropolitan Achievement Tests, and Stanford Achievement Tests.

Although I'll be drawing examples from these five tests, please remember that there are also many standardized achievement tests developed specifically for individual states. These tests are standardized in the sense that they are to be administered uniformly to the state's students and then scored in a predetermined manner. In most instances, state authorities had these customized achievement tests created so the test items would mesh better with the state's curricular emphases. Because most states now frame their curricular goals in the form of content standards—that is, the knowledge and skills students are supposed to master—a customized state test is occasionally referred to as a *standards-referenced* or a *standards-based* test. Sometimes, in an attempt to distinguish between a state test and one of the five most common standardized achievement tests used nationwide, the state-customized version is called a *criterion-referenced test*, while the nationally distributed tests are described as *norm-referenced tests.*

But what you need to know is that most of these state-customized standardized achievement tests were built by the very same companies that construct and market the five national standardized achievement tests. Consequently, many of the criticisms that can be leveled at the national tests can also be aimed quite accurately at statewide standardized achievement tests. In Chapter 5, you'll learn how to analyze the quality of any large-scale standardized achievement test—national, state, or even district-level. What I want you to understand at this point is that state-specific standardized achievement tests—although they may generate more public trust because they are adorned with all sorts of positive labels such as "our state's swell, customized, standards-based exam"—are not necessarily suitable for the purpose of evaluating educational quality. You'll need to determine the appropriateness of the high-stakes tests used in your own locale.

Standardized Testing's Origins and Measurement Mission

To understand the nature of today's standardized achievement tests, you need to know where they came from, and why. Fortunately, their origins are fairly easy to identify. And it's important for you to appreciate this assessment lineage because the original measurement mission of the very first standardized tests is, by and large, the same measurement mission that we see today's standardized achievement tests attempting to fulfill.

It all began during World War I, when the U.S. Army was called upon to field a fighting force of immense size. With all these new troops, the Army needed lots of new officers. How to determine which recruits were up to the challenge? Army officials were familiar with the individually administered intelligence test developed in 1905 by French psychologist Alfred Binet, but they recognized that with thousands of men needing to be tested, Binet's one-person-at-a-time testing approach wouldn't be practical. The Army then contacted the president of the American Psychological Association, Robert M. Yerkes, to see if his organization could devise a group-administrable test that would help identify the recruits most likely to succeed in the Army's officer training programs.

Yerkes appointed a committee of eight testing specialists to create a group aptitude test similar in its measurement mission to Binet's 1905 individual intelligence test. The committee convened in May 1917 at New Jersey's Vineland Training School. After a week of sustained effort, the committee created 10 different subtests, which, following several small-scale tryouts, became collectively known as the "Army Alpha."

As with Binet's individual intelligence tests, the Army Alpha was designed to discriminate among test-takers with respect to their intellectual abilities. In final form, the Alpha's subtests contained items requiring recruits to do such things as follow oral directions, identify appropriate analogies, reason mathematically, and choose appropriate synonyms or antonyms for selected vocabulary terms. The Army Alpha was exactly what it was intended to be: a group intelligence test.

The Alpha was administered to more than 1,700,000 men during World War I, and it worked wonderfully well. It determined where each new test-taker stood in relation to a collection of previous Alpha test-takers, known as the *norm group*. This comparative assessment approach allowed Army authorities to determine whether a recruit scored well (for example, at the 91st percentile) or not so well (for example, at the 35th percentile). The Alpha represented the first truly large-scale use of multiple-choice test items, and its items were subjected to all sorts of statistical analyses that allowed the test's five forms to do their comparative assessment job well.

Now, let's pause just a moment to make sure we're clear on the intent of the highly successful Army testing program. Put briefly, the Alpha was intended to permit comparisons among test-takers' relative intellectual abilities (as defined by the test's items). Based on recruits' comparative rankings, the Army could make reasonably accurate predictions about a recruit's likely success in a subsequent officer-training program. The Alpha, therefore, was a predictor test and, as such, was definitely an *aptitude* test.

Recruits who scored high on the Alpha were immediately sent to officer training facilities of one kind or another. Recruits who scored in the middle ranges were sent off to the trenches to fight the war. Recruits who scored very low on the test were urged to leave the service. All agreed that the Army Alpha testing program was a smashing success. Army officials were thoroughly satisfied with their aptitude test, and that satisfaction included both the Alpha's measurement rationale and the technical procedures used to create it.

Success sires emulation. Soon after World War I's conclusion, the U.S. Copyright Office received a substantial number of requests to copyright new educational tests. Almost without exception, these tests mimicked the Army Alpha's measurement strategy, which boiled down to making comparisons among test-takers by referencing their scores against the performances of a norm group. The Alpha assessment strategy, therefore, represented the first widespread use of a norm-referenced—that is, a comparative—testing approach.

Here's an important point: The educational tests that began to appear after World War I were not only intelligence-focused *aptitude* tests, like the Army Alpha, they were also *achievement* tests. For example, the first edition of today's Stanford Achievement Tests (now in their 9th edition) was published in 1923. Yes, the Army Alpha's assessment strategy became the template for almost all of this nation's subsequent standardized testing, irrespective of whether that testing was supposed to serve as an aptitude assessment or an achievement assessment.

And so it is that the overriding mission of today's standardized achievement tests is not fundamentally different from the mission of the Alpha: Develop a set of items that will allow for fine-grained and accurate comparisons among test-takers. Unfortunately, it is this mission that turns out to make standardized achievement tests altogether unsuitable for determining the effectiveness of teachers' instructional endeavors. Let's see why.

Two (Out of Three) Evaluative Shortcomings

Despite the widespread practice of using students' scores on standardized achievement tests to measure a school staff's instructional quality, there are three powerful reasons why this application of such tests is mistaken. I'll consider two of those reasons in this chapter, and the third reason in Chapter 4. (Reason 3 gets its own chapter because, in my view, it is not only the most compelling, it's the most complicated.)

As I describe each reason, I'll be referring chiefly to the five most widely used national standardized achievement tests, all of which are intended for use with elementary school children. Some of these tests also are designed to be used by secondary school students, in which case they are marketed under a different brand name. For example, the Riverside Publishing Company's Iowa Tests of Basic Skills for elementary children is transformed into that firm's Tests of Achievement and Proficiency designed for students in grades 9 through 12.

Whether intended for elementary or secondary students, the basic assessment approach reflected in national standardized achievement tests is fundamentally the same. And, as indicated earlier, that same assessment approach is often incorporated in state-customized achievement tests.

Reason 1: Teaching/Testing Mismatches

When the creators of national standardized achievement tests get down to their test-building activities, they encounter a messy curricular conundrum. Curricular content emphasized in one part of the United States is not necessarily emphasized in another. There may be substantial general similarities, but the curriculum that's endorsed in North Dakota, for instance, is not apt to coincide exactly with the curriculum favored in Michigan. Test publishers, mindful of the need to make their tests appropriate for diverse users, try to design items that mesh as well as possible with the diverse curricular preferences we find throughout the nation. Unfortunately, ample evidence has shown us that, as with clothing, a "one-size-fits-all" approach to curriculum often fails to be genuinely satisfying.

When officials of a given state, or even a particular school district, adopt one of the national standardized achievement tests, what's covered in the test may or may not be emphasized in the locally approved curriculum. And I'm not talking about a modest mismatch between the local curriculum and the content covered in the test. There are enormous and typically unrecognized mismatches between what's tested and what's taught. If you look carefully at what the items in a standardized achievement tests are actually measuring, you'll often find that *half or more of what's tested wasn't even supposed to be taught* in a particular district or state.

In a landmark study (Freeman et al., 1984) conducted in the early 1980s, researchers at Michigan State University made the reasonable assumption that the content of textbooks typically influences the content covered in classrooms. In their carefully controlled study, they compared the content of the nation's leading elementary mathematics textbooks with the content of the nation's leading standardized achievement tests. The investigators discovered that in the case of *every* standardized test, at least 50 percent of the content was not addressed meaningfully in *any* textbook. For some of the tests examined, fully 80 percent of the content was not addressed in more than a casual fashion by any textbook.

I realize that the Michigan State study is nearly two decades old, and I know that it deals with only one subject field at an elementary level. But I'd be willing to wager a year's supply of fudge brownies that if the study were replicated today at other grade levels and in other subject fields, the results would be remarkably similar. Here's why.

For one thing, a curricular cake can be cut in all sorts of ways. Even a skill as universally applauded as "reading comprehension" can be promoted through various methods and measured by strikingly different kinds of assessments. I've seen some teachers try to use graphic organizers (such as charts and graphs) to help children understand how the content of a reading selection is organized. I've also seen standardized achievement tests that asked students to demonstrate their reading comprehension by filling-in the blank sections of a partially completed graphic organizer. And have you ever seen students struggle with a *cloze* test, which attempts to assess a student's reading comprehension skill by seeing whether the student can supply the missing words in paragraphs from which every fifth word has been deleted?

There are also all sorts of conventional ways of teaching and testing students' abilities to comprehend what they read. Given the diversity of curricular conceptions of reading comprehension and the myriad measurement tactics that can be used to tell whether students possess the skill, it's obvious that there will be many instances in which a teaching approach and a testing approach may pass one another in the night. Mismatches are very common.

But there's one more reality-based explanation for the frequent mismatch between teaching and testing, and it's related to children's attention spans. Measurement people might be willing to test students for three or four hours at a crack, but they recognize that few elementary school students share this enthusiasm. Therefore, to limit test administration sessions to an hour or so, the creators of standardized achievement tests must sample from the complete array of skills and knowledge they regard as eligible for assessment at any grade level.

Think, for example, about the substantial amount of content that a 6th grader ought to have learned during a year's worth of study in language arts or in mathematics. It's unrealistic to try to assess *all* of that content. The test developer must make choices about what to test, and often, these choices will not mesh with the curricular emphases in a given state or district. To illustrate, from 25 or 30 significant mathematics skills identified nationally for 5th graders, the test's publishers may opt to assess only 21. Those 21 math skills may or may not be in line with the 17 math skills stressed in the local educators' instruction.

These kinds of serious mismatches are seldom recognized by local educators or by local educational policymakers. Mismatches go undetected largely because local educators fail to subject national tests to an item-by-item scrutiny. In their view, national tests are not modifiable, so why should they spend time looking at the test's items?

But as you'll read in the next chapter, an item review is pivotal in determining whether the standardized achievement test is really suitable for evaluating instruction in a given educational setting. Tests are made up of items. Unless you rigorously scrutinize a test's items, you'll never really understand what the test is assessing. And you'll never recognize if a teaching/testing mismatch is present. How fair is it to use test content to judge the quality of a group of teachers when 50 percent or more of that content wasn't even supposed to be taught by the school's staff?

Summing up, here is the initial reason we should not allow educational quality to be determined by students' scores on standardized tests:

Standardized achievement tests should not be used to evaluate the quality of students' schooling because there are meaningful mismatches between what is tested and what is supposed to be taught, and those mismatches are often unrecognized.

Reason 2: The Tendency to Jettison Items Covering Important Content

I attribute Reason 2 to the "Army Alpha thinking" displayed by most of today's measurement specialists. Remember, the Alpha worked well because it was able to produce a substantial degree of *score-spread* among examinees. If the Alpha's scores weren't spread out widely enough, then different recruits couldn't be contrasted with sufficient precision to distinguish between men who scored at the 83rd or 84th percentiles. The fine-grained comparisons, and the score-spread necessary to produce them, are at the heart of the Army Alpha approach to assessment, which, as noted, remains the underlying assessment approach favored by today's standardized achievement test creators.

The other factor that spurs the developers of standardized achievement tests to covet substantial score-spread is related to the technical determination of a test's *reliability*. Test publishers can compute three different kinds of reliability, all of which are rooted in the concept of *consistency*. The most commonly calculated kind of reliability refers to the consistency with which a test's items measure whatever they're measuring. But all three types of reliability will be higher if the test produces substantial score-spread. The better the score-spread, the higher the test's reliability. This occurs because the ways of calculating reliability are correlationally based, and substantial score-spread is required for high correlation—that is, reliability coefficiencies.

And why is high reliability so esteemed by the measurement staffs who create standardized achievement tests? It's simple: *High reliability sells tests.* When it comes time to select among competing standardized achievement tests, the decision makers (say, a district or state test-selection committee) will look to many evaluative factors to determine which test is best. They may give attention to the degree of apparent alignment between published descriptions of the test's content and the locally sanctioned curricular content. The decision makers usually consider the efforts made to eliminate from the test any content that might be biased against minorities. And they always pay attention to evidence regarding the test's technical qualities, one of which is reliability.

Other factors being equal, a test that has better reliability than any of the other tests will be chosen over its competitors. Thus, test developers diligently seek high indicators of reliability and the score-spread that helps create such high reliability. Substantial score-spread not only contributes to more accurate discriminations among examinees, it also helps peddle tests. And well-peddled tests make more money for the shareholders in the corporations that build and sell standardized tests.

Now let's turn our attention to an important technical point about the nature of test items that contribute most effectively to the creation of score-spread. These are the test items that are answered correctly by roughly 50 percent of the examinees. Test folks use the term "*p*-value" to indicate the percentage of students who answer an item correctly. An item with a *p*-value of .85 would have been answered correctly by 85 percent of those who attempted to answer it. A test item answered correctly by exactly half the examinees would have a *p*-value of .50.

Items that make the best contribution to a test's score-spread are those with *p*-values in the .40 to .60 range. Not surprisingly, most items on the national standardized achievement tests have *p*-values in that range. Items that have higher *p*-values—for example, .80 or .90—are rarely included in these tests, having been determined during shakedown trials to be "too easy." Moreover, any items that produce unanticipated high *p*-values are almost always removed from a standardized test once the test is revised (typically every 5–10 years). A test item with a *p*-value of .93 just doesn't make a sufficiently substantial contribution to the production of score-spread. Indeed, an item that *all* examinees answered correctly would have a *p*-value of 1.00 and would make *zero* contribution to the creation of score-spread. Useless!

Now for the difficulty created by this relentless quest for score-spread. As it turns out, teachers tend to stress the curricular content they believe to be most important. The more significant a topic, the more likely it is that the teacher will emphasize the topic instructionally. And, of course, the more that teachers emphasize any curricular content, the better that students are likely to perform on items measuring such content. As a perverse consequence, items covering the most important things that teachers teach tend to be excluded from standardized achievement tests. Such items, even though they tap teacher-stressed content, will either not have been placed on the test to begin with, or will be discarded from the test at revision (as a consequence of high p-values).

Thus, the more important the content, the more likely teachers are to stress it. The more that teachers stress important content, the better that students will do on an item measuring that content. But the better that students do on such an item, the more likely it is that the item will disappear from the test. How fair is it, then, to evaluate a school's staff on the basis of a test that, because of its Army Alpha-like quest for score-spread, fails to include items covering the most important things teachers are trying to teach? And, of course, those important things will typically be the things that teachers have taught well.

The second reason, then, that standardized achievement tests should not be used to evaluate educational quality is somewhat technical, but nonetheless important:

> **Standardized achievement tests should not be used to evaluate the quality of students' schooling because the quest for wide score-spread tends to eliminate items covering important content that teachers have emphasized and students have mastered.**

These two reasons—teaching/testing mismatches and the tendency to eliminate the very items covering the most important things that teachers teach—*all by themselves* should be sufficient to disincline anyone from using students' scores on standardized achievement tests as indicators of instructional quality.

But there's a third reason, one that in my mind is far nastier. It's the reason you'll learn about in the next chapter. And it's a reason that becomes clear only when you look carefully at the kinds of test items actually used on standardized achievement tests. Taken together, the two reasons in this chapter and the one in Chapter 4 form a potent three-point rationale for *never* using standardized achievement tests to judge educational quality.

Confounded Causality

WHEN POLICYMAKERS CREATE ACCOUNTABILITY SYSTEMS CENTERED ON STU-
dents' test scores, they assume that higher test scores reflect better
instruction. Typically, state or district officials administer high-stakes
test to students in certain grades at the same time each year. Then
the scores of this year's 6th graders, for example, are compared with
the scores of last year's 6th graders. If scores go up from one year to
the next, officials conclude that instruction has been effective. If
scores stay the same, or go down from one year to the next, then we
are asked to believe that instruction was not effective.

The whole strategy of basing instructional evaluations on shifts
in students' test scores depends on the proposition that differing levels of instructional effectiveness will produce related levels of student test performance. Is that proposition defensible?

Most of us understand why it's unproductive to try to compare
apples and oranges. It is every bit as inane to compare the test

performances of two sets of substantially different students. When I was a high school teacher, it was abundantly clear to me when one year's freshman class was more (or less) intellectually able than the previous year's freshman class. Actually, the first year that I taught, my 9th grade freshman students were quite sharp. The following year, I detected an obvious drop-off in the cerebral capabilities of my new freshman class. Had I been teaching in a high-stakes testing environment, any reasonable kind of achievement test administered at the end of the second school year would have shown that my 9th graders' test scores had gone down from one year to the next. Would that have meant I was doing a poor instructional job? Of course not. The kids were different.

And that, of course, is one of the serious drawbacks of making year-to-year comparisons of test scores. The caliber of the students fluctuates. This year's 8th graders may be super-swift in contrast to last year's somewhat slow 8th graders. Does a year-to-year increase in 8th graders' test scores signify splendid teaching? Clearly, the answer is no.

For year-to-year comparisons of students' test scores to yield defensible interpretations, the composition of each year's students needs to be essentially the same. It is true that the ability levels of each year's crop of students at any given grade level are likely to be more similar to each other than they are to the ability levels found at other grade levels. That's especially true if you were to consider an entire state or an entire nation. However, in a *particular* district, and especially within a *specific* school, the students' cognitive quality at a given grade level can vary substantially from one year to the next.

Accordingly, attempts to derive insights about teachers' effectiveness based on year-to-year comparisons of their students' scores on springtime standardized achievement tests are often destined to fail, simply because this year's apples are different from last year's nectarines. Given the difficulties arising from the variability of students, some policymakers think that they can circumvent such problems by studying the *same* children from year to year. In many localities, the high costs of assessment preclude annual testing at all grade levels. However, let's assume there's a state that gives an annual test in early May to all students, using the appropriate grade-level form of the same standardized achievement test. It is possible, therefore, to see how Margie Johnson scores each spring on the same supposedly grade-appropriate test.

Unfortunately, there's a problem with this approach, too: It is impossible to devise truly *equally difficult* test forms for each grade level. When Margie Johnson earns a 59th percentile this year in contrast to a 55th percentile last year, does this really signify that Margie has made a 4-percent gain in achievement? We just can't say.

Here's where people's deference to standardized achievement testers once again gets in the way of clear thinking. Although a lot of folks believe otherwise, these tests are simply not precise enough to capture meaningful data that demonstrate year-to-year changes in an individual student's educational achievements. Consider the inherent obstacle of making sure that the collection of 55 test items children will face on this year's 6th grade test presents the same degree of age-appropriate challenge as the collection of 55 items they faced last year on the 5th grade test and will face next year on the 7th grade test. A test company's statisticians may go through all sorts of gyrations to set up identical grade-to-grade increases in each test's degree of difficulty, but they really can't do so with the needed level of precision.

In the last chapter, I pointed out that the first reason standardized achievement tests should not be used to evaluate educational quality is that there are often major mismatches between content assessed and content taught. But the degree of mismatch surely varies from year to year. At any given school, the 4th grade form of a standardized achievement test may contain a lot more or a lot less of the locally stressed curriculum than the 5th grade form does. Even if we were able to study the same children's year-to-year performances on "equidifficult" test forms, these kinds of dissimilarities in assessment-instruction alignment would contaminate the clarity with which same-student test gains could be studied, and would prevent us from making valid inferences about instructional quality.

The problems of year-to-year comparisons of students' test scores, whether focused on different students or on the same students, are so substantial that such contrasts should be undertaken with great caution. But suppose we could somehow find a way to make sensible year-to-year comparisons of a student's standardized achievement test scores. Would it then be okay to use those scores to evaluate educational quality? No, and I'll tell you why. A student's test *score* is determined by the student's responses to the test's *items*. Most folks believe that the items on a standardized achievement test measure what a student learns in school. If Michael's teachers (and Michael's school) have done an effective job, Michael will have learned the content presented on the standardized achievement test and will respond correctly to the test items. But this is not how it works at all.

The items on standardized achievement tests measure a variety of things—and not just what a student should have learned in school. Putting it more precisely, three distinct factors determine whether a student will correctly answer the items on a standardized achievement test. These factors are (1) what the student learned in school, (2) the student's socioeconomic status, and (3) the student's inherited academic aptitudes.

To illustrate my argument as clearly as possible, I am going to present a series of actual test items from one of today's widely used national standardized achievement tests. Although I've modified the items slightly to maintain test security, I have not altered the nature of the intellectual task each item presents. In other words, the *cognitive demands* of all the items you'll see in this chapter are just as they are on the actual test. To reduce any test-taking anxieties you may possess, I've indicated the correct answers with a little check mark.

What the Student Learned in School

Let's start off by looking at some items that do what they're suppose to do and measure what they're supposed to measure: the kinds of skills and knowledge we hope children will be learning in school. Consider the 4th grade mathematics item in Figure 4.1, designed to measure a student's ability to *estimate*.

I think we all agree that the ability to make mathematical estimations is a useful skill, one that we employ all the time in our daily lives. Fittingly, it's a skill taught in most school districts. Provided this sort of estimation is covered in the 4th grade curriculum, then the item in Figure 4.1 seems fine to me.

4.1 **A 4th Grade Mathematics Item**

Todd earns between $7 and $11 daily from an afterschool job. *About* how many days will Todd need to work to earn $90?

A. 5
B. 10 ✔
C. 15
D. 20

Now let's look at the 6th grade spelling item in Figure 4.2. The student is presented with three sentences. One word in each sentence is designated as potentially misspelled. The student's task is to spot the spelling mistake (if there is one) or indicate that no spelling error is present.

We want children to learn how to spell correctly, and this sort of item seems to be a proper assessment of an important language arts skill. If the designated words coincide with the spelling words

---

4.2 **A 6th Grade Spelling Item**

Identify the spelling error, if there is one.

A. We found her **luggage.**
B. I **perswaded** him to join us. ✔
C. The water **faucet** was dripping.
D. No spelling error.

---

taught to the 6th grade test-takers, then I'd say the Figure 4.2 spelling item is a good one. It taps what kids should be taught. And if it coincides with what 6th grade teachers at a particular school are supposed to be teaching, then it's a good illustration of an item that helps measure what children should have learned in school.

Before we move on, though, recall from Chapter 3 the second reason standardized achievement tests shouldn't be used to evaluate educational quality: *There's a tendency to remove from standardized achievement tests any item on which students perform too well.* If there are *really* important words that 6th graders need to learn how to spell, then many 6th grade teachers will focus their instruction on such words. Yet if too many students succeed in spelling any of these words—for example, if a spelling word has a *p*-value of .92—then it's very unlikely that such a word will remain on the test. Because these words have been taught so well, they've now become "too easy" to be included in a national standardized achievement test. Instead, the test developers will usually opt to select words that are less well-taught, words that turn out to have mid-level *p*-values between .40 and .60, *words that will provide score-spread.*

To recap, one of the three kinds of items you'll find on a standardized achievement test focuses directly on what's taught in school. If all the items on such tests were of this sort, there would be far less cause for concern. (We'd only have to worry about the degree of measurement misalignment with a particular curriculum.) But there are two other kinds of items on standardized achievement tests that have little to do with any appraisal of a school staff's effectiveness.

The Student's Socioeconomic Status

A second kind of item you'll encounter on a standardized achievement test is the kind that's more likely to be answered correctly by children from affluent and middle-class families than by children from low-income families. These are the items that are clearly linked to a child's *socioeconomic status* (SES)—that is, the probability that an individual student will answer the item correctly will be meaningfully influenced by such factors as parental education levels and family income. And those two factors, of course, lead to all sorts of other things that can influence a child's response to a test item.

Look at the information in Figure 4.3 regarding how much money it will take to support a child born in 1999 from birth to age 17. According to this estimate, based on U.S. Department of Agriculture data, low-income families will dish out almost $120,000 and upper-income families will spend more than $230,000 to get their child-rearing accomplished. And these expenditures focus only on *necessities*. In other words, the costs listed in Figure 4.3 do not include all the frills that kids from middle- and upper-income families routinely receive. If the numbers included such things as trips to Disneyland or summer vacations at Camp Lakeside, the cost differentials would be far more dramatic. Do kids from higher-SES backgrounds have an advantage when it comes to the kinds of experiences and information often incorporated in standardized achievement tests? You bet they do!

Children from upper- and middle-class families are more likely to grow up in a home environment rich in the sorts of materials and experiences that will substantially benefit them when it comes time

4.3 Family Costs for Supporting a Child (Born in 1999) through Age 17

Family Income Level	Average Amount Spent on Food, Shelter, & Other Necessities
Low Income	$117,390
Middle Income	$160,140
Upper Income	$233,850

(*Source of data*: U.S. Department of Agriculture [2000, April 27]. *Expenditures on children by families*. Washington, DC: Author.)

to do battle with a standardized achievement test. In these homes, you're likely to encounter the kinds of books, newspapers, and magazines that often form the basis of test items on standardized achievement tests. You're also likely to find access to cable television, such as The History Channel or The Discovery Channel. Programs on these networks are unavailable to a child whose low-income parents can't afford the expense of cable TV. And a good many items on standardized achievement tests contain key content that frequently pops up on such educationally oriented cable channels.

In the homes of affluent and well-educated parents, standard American English is likely to be spoken. Children of these parents grow up routinely hearing the words and phrases that form the items on standardized achievement tests. That's especially true if the test deals with language arts, where you'll find item after item in which the child who grew up in a family where "proper" English was used has a tremendous leg up over children whose parents' first language wasn't English or whose parents spoke English in a "nonstandard" manner.

I now live on the island of Kauai in Hawaii. Numerous Hawaii-born people are almost bilingual in the sense that they can use standard English and also pidgin (a simplified form of English with a markedly reduced vocabulary). But for many of Hawaii's children, the primary language spoken in the home is pidgin. What happens when one of these youngsters encounters language arts items on a standardized achievement test requiring the identification of appropriate grammar, spelling, or punctuation? I hope you can see how a child from a pidgin-spoken-here family is likely to have a much tougher task in answering those language arts items than a child whose parents normally speak in the kinds of sentences that are featured on the test—and featured, of course, as the correct answers!

These test-taking disadvantages also face children whose parents were born in Vietnam, Mexico, Romania, or any other non-English speaking country. And the same disadvantages face children growing up in parts of Appalachia, inner city Detroit, or any other community where nonstandard English is the norm. If a standardized achievement test's items are peppered with forms of a language the child doesn't routinely hear at home, that child will be decisively disadvantaged when dealing with certain items on that test.

If you've been thinking about what you've been reading, you may be wondering why the folks who construct standardized achievement tests would ever do such a silly thing as include a flock of SES-linked items in their tests. Indeed, you may be wondering if this is simply a case of undetected assessment bias.

I'll give you hint: Think about the Army Alpha heritage of today's standardized achievement tests. Remember that the Alpha and its successor tests were designed to produce a sufficient degree of score-spread, all the better to permit the fine-grained contrasts that are at the heart of the comparative approach to measurement. If you think hard about SES, you'll realize that it is a nicely spread-out variable—and it's a variable that isn't easily altered. Ordinarily, it takes a generation or two for families to make significant increases or decreases in their SES standings. As a consequence, a standardized test item that is meaningfully linked to SES will help spread out examinees' scores. It's impossible to get around: SES items are deeply useful in this form of testing.

"Useful? Useful for whom?" you'd be right to sputter here. Yes, the presence of SES-linked items means students from middle- and upper-SES backgrounds will tend to do better on standardized achievement tests than will students who come from lower-SES backgrounds. According to the current conceptions of accountability, it means teachers who work with a group of high-SES children will tend to receive higher evaluations of instructional effectiveness than will teachers who work with lower-SES children. Obviously, it is both inaccurate and unfair to evaluate a school staff on the basis of its students' scores on standardized achievement tests if those tests contain many SES-linked items. And believe me, those tests do. Ready for some examples?

Sample SES-Linked Items

As with the items presented earlier, this collection of test items has been only modestly massaged from actual items I found in one of today's standardized achievement tests. At first glance, many appear to be appropriate for assessing students' achieved skills and knowledge within designated subject fields. But if you look more closely, you'll detect in each item the subtle but very real presence of SES-linked content that gives an edge to children whose parents are middle- or upper-class, whose parents are fairly well-off financially, and whose parents have been on the receiving end of at least some post-secondary schooling. Let's begin with the 6th grade science item in Figure 4.4.

4.4   A 6th Grade Science Item

If you wanted to find out if another planet had mountains or rivers, which of these tools should you use?

A. a pair of binoculars
B. a telescope ✔
C. a microscope
D. a camera

It should be obvious that a 6th grade child whose parents own a telescope would have an easier time with this item than would a child who didn't have a telescope in the house. Similarly, if you were a child whose parents watched and discussed cable TV programs about astronomy, you'd have an edge over children from homes that couldn't afford cable TV.

You see, even if there had been *some* instructional attention given in 5th grade or 6th grade science to the four options cited in the item, youngsters from more affluent families are almost certain to find this item easier because it will mesh more directly with their out-of-school experiences. It's not that a child from a low-income family will *never* be able to answer this science item correctly. But if you were to contrast the performances of 100 advantaged children and 100 disadvantaged children on an item like the one in Figure 4.4, it's pretty clear which group, *on average*, would be correct more often.

Now take a look at the 4th grade reading item in Figure 4.5, an example of a common type of item intended to determine whether students can figure out what a word with multiple meanings actually means in a particular context.

4.5   A 4th Grade Reading Item

My father's <u>field</u> is computer graphics.
In which of the sentences below does the word <u>field</u> mean the same thing as in the sentence above?

A. The shortstop knew how to <u>field</u> his position.
B. We prepared the <u>field</u> by plowing it.
C. What <u>field</u> do you plan to enter when you graduate? ✔
D. The nurse examined my <u>field</u> of vision.

Here, the item's cognitive demand requires the test-taker to figure out what the word *field* means. But consider that children from families in which one or both parents are professionals—dentists, lawyers, or journalists, for example—are likely to have an easier time with this item than will children from families where the mother cleans other people's homes and the father works in a car wash. People who clean houses or wash cars for a living rarely think of themselves as having a "field" of employment. Probably, children whose parents have what society regards as fields of employment will do better on the item in Figure 4.5 than will children whose parents' work falls outside that designation.

Now consider the 6th grade language arts item in Figure 4.6, where the student must pick out a mistake, if there is one.

4.6 A 6th Grade Language Arts Item

George winds up and threw **the ball to the catcher.**

Which words are correct for this sentence?

A. up, and threw
B. up and will throw
C. up and throws ✔
D. no mistake

To select the correct answer, the child must recognize that the past-tense of the verb "throw" doesn't match the present-tense of the verb "winds." Of course, we'd like all children to be able to use consistent verb tenses. But 6th graders whose families routinely speak in a manner that uses parallel-tense verbs will be far more likely to answer this item correctly than will 6th graders who seldom if ever hear their family members use matching-tense verbs.

Next, look at the 5th grade language arts item in Figure 4.7.

4.7 A 5th Grade Language Arts Item

Jamal found one full issue of *Animals Magazine* that contained only articles about tigers. One of the writers in the magazine had studied tigers for 25 years and had written many books about tigers. Where in the magazine would Jamal be *most* likely to find the titles of these books?

A. On the back of the magazine's title page.
B. In the biographical information at the end of that author's article. ✔
C. In the table of contents that lists all of the magazine's articles.
D. In an earlier issue of *Animals Magazine*.

Clearly, a child growing up in a family where magazines are available and often read will be more likely to know where someone might look for a listing of an author's other books. Actually, I think this is a weak item, because there are many magazines in which "the biographical information at the end of the article" does *not* contain the titles of an author's other books. But a child who has had a lot of at-home exposure to magazines (especially to child-appropriate magazines supplied by parents who can afford to buy them) will know that answer options A, C, and D are definitely not correct. Consequently, this child will be more likely to opt for the correct answer.

Now, examine the 6th grade science item in Figure 4.8.

4.8   A 6th Grade Science Item

A plant's fruit always contains seeds. Which of the items below is <u>not</u> a fruit?

A. orange
B. pumpkin
C. apple
D. celery ✔

Here's a simple, short quiz just for you: Looking back at the item in Figure 4.8, who is more likely to answer it correctly, Child A or Child B?

• Child A's parents often buy fresh celery at the supermarket, and each Halloween, the family carves a jack-o'-lantern from a fresh pumpkin.

• Child B's parents are getting by on food stamps, never buy fresh celery, and can't afford to purchase fresh pumpkins at Halloween.

Yes, the item in Figure 4.8 is an SES-linked item, and a pretty blatant one. Remember, *I'm not making these up*. In slightly different form, all these items actually appear in a national standardized achievement test.

For a final example of an SES-linked item, look at the 5th grade language arts item in Figure 4.9. It is intended to help determine if the child knows the proper use of the pronouns "I" and "me." It also illustrates an important point about how our strong beliefs about what children *should* be learning can sometimes permit SES-linked items to go undetected.

4.9   **A 5th Grade Language Arts Item**

Our music teacher was surprised when | Jill and me sang | **the wrong note.**

Which are the correct words for this sentence?

A. Jill and me sung
B. Jill and I will sing
C. Jill and I sang ✔
D. No mistake

Personally, I find the misuse of "I" and "me" particularly grating. If a friend says, "He gave the check to Jack and I," I cringe. I *want* folks to know it should be "Jack and me." I *want* kids to be able to answer the item in Figure 4.9 correctly. But as much as I yearn for children to use the nominative and objective cases of the first-person pronoun correctly, I have to admit that the item in Figure 4.9 simply reeks of SES bias. Kids from families in which "I" and "me" are routinely used properly will, on average, do much better on this item than will kids from families where "I" and "me" are frequently misused.

Does this mean that all low-SES children will miss this item, while all high-SES children will get it right? Of course not. But as with all the sample items I've presented in this section, the *probability* of high-SES students' getting more correct answers than low-SES students is, to me, indisputable. And that's why evaluating schools on the basis of a standardized achievement test that contains many such SES-linked items is inaccurate, unfair, and patently indefensible.

The Problem's Prevalence

You should quite properly be wondering whether the SES-linked items I've shown you are the exceptions, and whether, in reality, there are relatively few such items on today's standardized achievement tests. It's an appropriate question, and being a proactive and remarkably responsive author, I'm going to supply you with an on-target answer.

First, I haven't analyzed *all* the items on *all* of today's standardized achievement tests. However, over the past few years, my research into assessment has led me to devote a lot of time to test-item scrutiny. I really feel fairly foolish for not having done so many years ago. After all, *items* are the things that lead to high or low test scores, and they demand rigorous inspection.

At any rate, on several occasions during the past few years, I've gone through an entire grade-level's worth of several of the five national standardized achievement tests. My objective: Review each item and, as objectively as possible, determine whether that item is SES-linked. In Figure 4.10, I provide a summary of my findings—approximate percentage of SES-linked items I found per subject, based on the average counts from my item-by-item review of two national tests, at one grade level each.

As you see, the number of SES-linked items varies according to the subject matter being tested. My counts always turned up more SES-linked items in the language arts sections of the tests and fewer in the math sections. Clearly, the percentages of SES-linked items would also vary from grade level to grade level and from test to test. Some tests surely have fewer SES-linked items; some tests, I fear, may have more. Perhaps you're thinking that, although I tried to be objective, I may have been too tough on the two grade-level's worth of test items I reviewed. But even if you were to divide these percentages in half, three of the four content areas would still have what I regard as unacceptably high proportions of SES-linked items.

I want you to realize that I'm not talking about an isolated item or two. There are many, many SES-linked items in today's standardized achievement tests. These items do a fantastic job of spreading out examinees' scores, but they do a miserable job of helping evaluate a school staff's real effectiveness. Even a few standardized achievement test items answered correctly or incorrectly can make a substantial difference in a school's relative ranking. Now, let's take a look at the third factor that determines how an individual student will respond to standardized test items.

4.10 **Percentages of Items Judged to Be Linked to Socioeconomic Status**

Subject	% SES Items
Reading	15%
Language Arts	65%
Mathematics	5%
Science	45%
Social Studies	45%

The Student's Inherited Academic Aptitude

From an educator's perspective, and surely from a parent's point of view, it would be delightful if all children were born with precisely the same amount of intellectual potential. Nobody would have to worry about who was smarter than whom. Parental expectations for siblings could be fairly similar. We could confidently and correctly attribute the differences in students' achievement to their levels of effort or to the quality of the instruction provided by their teachers.

For both teachers and parents, life would be far easier if kids were all born with identical potentials. But they aren't.

Genetic inheritance plays a prominent role in determining how easy it is for children to acquire certain kinds of skills. Some youngsters are, from birth, more adept athletically. Some youngsters are more facile in dealing with quantitative concepts. Some are better able to handle verbal complexities. I am definitely not suggesting that a child's gene pool will exclusively determine that child's future. Most research suggests that both nature and nurture share equally in determining a person's successes or failures. But I am suggesting that children inherit different amounts of different kinds of aptitudes.

Howard Gardner's view that there are multiple kinds of intelligence makes a good deal of sense to me. Some people are born with more aesthetic potential; others are born with more logical-mathematical potential (Gardner, 1994). This certainly appears to be the case within my own family. I have four children, and they differ from one another quite substantially in their verbal, quantitative, and spatial perceptions. My daughter is super with words but sad with numbers. My sons are much more adept at spatial visualization. And my children have differed from the get-go.

Recognizing that children differ in their verbal, spatial, and quantitative potentials, the creators of standardized achievement tests toss in a number of items that measure such aptitudes. These test items appear to be assessing what children should have learned in subject areas such as social studies, science, or math. But if you analyze carefully what the *cognitive demands* of the items are—that is, what those items are really asking students to do—you'll discover that the item is fundamentally measuring the academic potentials that children were fortunate or unfortunate to have inherited from their parents: inborn word-smarts, number-smarts, and spatial-smarts.

If you were to consider one of these items all by itself, you'd likely conclude that it was ideally suited to function on an intelligence test. You'd be right. Indeed, more *achievement* test items than most people imagine are thinly camouflaged *intelligence* test items. And why would standardized achievement tests contain items that measure inherited academic aptitudes? If you've been thinking about what you've read so far in this and the preceding chapter, you probably have an answer ready.

That's right: Items measuring inherited academic aptitudes do a dandy job at producing the score-spread that's at the heart of standardized testing. Children's inherited aptitudes are nicely dispersed. And, by definition, such inherited potentials are unalterable. Sure, a numerical numbskull may become reasonably good in arithmetic by working hard at it, but the person's initial aptitude for quantitative accomplishments hasn't changed. It's just that some people capitalize more fully on their inborn potentials than do others. And items based on such inherited aptitudes help provide the cherished score-spread that's been sought by test developers since the days of the Army Alpha.

Sample Aptitude-Linked Items

I have another half-dozen items to present, again pulled with insignificant alterations from one of the current national standardized achievement tests. Please analyze the items carefully, thinking about whether the item focuses more directly on what ought to be learned in school or on what a child picked up in the gene pool sweepstakes. Again, don't be misdirected by whether you'd *like* children to be able to answer these sorts of items correctly. Clearly, we all would like students to perform wonderfully on all tests. But the issue now before us is whether such test items should be used to evaluate *the quality of instruction* that our children receive.

Let's begin with the 6th grade social studies item in Figure 4.11.

4.11 A 6th Grade Social Studies Item

If someone really wants to conserve resources, one good way to do so is to

A. leave lights on even if they are not needed.
B. wash small loads instead of large loads in a clothes-washing machine.
C. write on both sides of a piece of paper. ✔
D. place used newspapers in the garbage.

This item may look like it's measuring social studies content, because it refers to the conservation of resources, but it could have come straight from the Army Alpha. It's an intelligence-type item, based substantially on a child's inherited verbal aptitude.

A verbally adroit child will have no trouble figuring out the correct answer here. By reading the "stem" of the item (the part preceding the answer choices), the child will discern that the key phrase is "conserve resources." Kids who are born word-smart can identify such things pretty easily. And that same sort of verbally facile child will have no trouble translating "conserve resources" into "save." Having done so, the word-smart child will then review each of the four answer options and realize that three of them have nothing to do with *saving*. The child will choose Option C, not because of what was taught in school, but because the child was born with a solid chunk of verbal aptitude.

Look now at the 3rd grade mathematics item in Figure 4.12.

4.12 A 3rd Grade Mathematics Item

The secret number is inside the circle. It is also inside the square.
It is NOT inside the triangle.

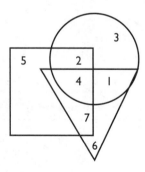

Which of these is the secret number?

A. 2 ✔   B. 3   C. 4   D. 7

This item measures both inherited quantitative aptitude and inherited verbal aptitude. Notice that to figure out the "secret number," a 3rd grader needs to mentally keep track of the statements above the circle-square-triangle figure. Kids who were born with lots of number-smarts will have an easier time with this sort of mental place-holding task than will kids who were born with lesser number-smarts. Moreover, assuming equivalent number-smarts, children who can keep track of the item's verbal components—that is, children who were born with more word-smarts—will most likely do better on this item than will children who have trouble remembering the item's verbal directives.

And let me ask you this: How important is it for human beings to develop the skill of finding secret numbers in overlapping geometric shapes? I can't think of a single time in my life when this real-world quandary presented itself to me. Don't you think teachers ought to be focusing on more useful material? But, because of this item's heavy reliance on inherited academic aptitudes, you can be sure that it will help create a delightfully spread-out set of test scores. So the item remains.

Figure 4.13 shows an item for 2nd graders that is obviously aimed at measuring children's inborn spatial-visualization aptitude.

4.13 A 2nd Grade Mathematics Item

Teacher: "Look at the box on the left with the arrow pointing at it. Suppose you turned that box upside down. Which of the boxes at the right would it look like?"

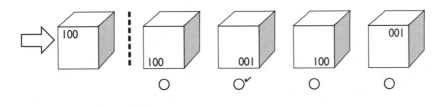

Does 2nd grade strike you as a little young for standardized achievement testing? As you may know, most test publishers distribute standardized achievement tests designed for children as young as 1st graders. Some also dispense tests for kindergarten children. One wonders whether some day we will see the emergence of prenatal achievement tests! This would, at any rate, determine once and for all which test items were measuring inborn aptitude.

Because inborn spatial visualization potential is nicely dispersed in the population, the spatial-aptitude item in Figure 4.13 will produce a psychometrically satisfying score-spread. But why would a teacher ever want to teach this? Picture a 2nd grade teacher who asks her 8-year-olds to "Take part, boys and girls, in today's mental box-turning exercises." Absurd!

Even though it clearly doesn't measure what's taught in school, the item in Figure 4.13 will spread students' scores. In addition, it *looks* mathematical. So there it sits in a 2nd grade standardized achievement test, doing its score-spreading thing. I hope you see that this doesn't make the item suitable for judging the quality of schooling.

Figure 4.14 shows a 6th grade social studies item dealing with inventions, a frequent focus in social studies instruction. Today's standardized achievement tests typically contain 50 or so social studies items, and this one would seem to fit in nicely.

4.14   A 6th Grade Social Studies Item

One of the following inventions has helped farmers in the production of food. Which invention is it?

A. the vacuum cleaner
B. the automatic clothes-washing machine
C. the camera
D. the plow ✔

Think about what this item really asks students to do. They must consider four inventions to determine which one has a meaningful relationship to food production. The child who inherited a bigger dose of word-smarts will figure out that the first three inventions, while commendable on other grounds, don't have anything to do with food production. Word-smart 6th graders will be able to identify the final choice, *plow,* as an invention that helps people plant stuff that grows—certain kinds of food, for instance. Although this item appears suitable for a social studies achievement test, again, what it's really measuring is intelligence.

The item in Figure 4.15 is intended to see whether 6th graders can work with numbers in their heads. The cognitive demand presented here could be handled algebraically, but it could also be solved by engaging in a little mental number-swapping to see which numbers need to be switched so that all three equations will end up equaling six. Kids with inborn number-smarts are almost certain to do reasonably well on this item. Kids with less number-smarts may be baffled.

4.15 A 6th Grade Mathematics Item

Look at the three division problems below. The same number will belong in all three answer circles if two of the boxed numbers trade places.

$\boxed{12} \div \boxed{6} = \bigcirc$

$\boxed{18} \div \boxed{3} = \bigcirc$

$\boxed{36} \div \boxed{2} = \bigcirc$

Which two numbers should be traded so that all three division problems have the same answer?

A. Trade the 3 and 18.
B. Trade the 3 and 6.
C. Trade the 6 and 18.
D. Trade the 2 and 6. ✔

This task looks mathematical, all right, but how practical is the mathematics involved? Have you ever been required to do anything remotely resembling the number-trading task called for here? But the item will almost certainly contribute to score-spread.

For my final example of an item measuring inherited academic aptitude, take a gander at the 3rd grade reading item in Figure 4.16. The test-taker is supposed to figure out the meaning of the word "suspend" from the context of the sentence in which it is found. It's obvious that kids who already know what the word "suspend" means won't have any difficulty in coming up with the correct answer. Among those who don't know the word's definition, a child born with ample word-smarts will be more likely to figure out that three of the answer options don't mesh with the rest of the sentence that's given in the item's stem. The word-smart child will simply try out the four answer options in the stem and see that only one works fairly well. This looks like a reading item, but it functions like an intelligence item.

4.16   A 3rd Grade Reading Item

Jordan will suspend the flag from the roof, so everybody can see it.
What does *suspend* mean?

A. hide
B. pull
C. hang ✔
D. sneak

More Frightening Proportions

You've now reviewed six items that chiefly measure students' inherited academic aptitudes. I found them all, in only slightly different form, in one of today's national standardized achievement tests. Are there many such items in these tests? Guess who kept track during his recent, objective-as-possible, item-by-item analysis of a pair of current national standardized achievement tests. Figure 4.17 shows my findings—the approximate percentages of items for which inherited academic aptitude was the *dominant* factor influencing a student's likelihood of answering correctly. Those proportions of inheritance-influenced items are, in my view, whopping! And even if I was too stringent in my judgments, even if you chopped these percentages in half, they'd still be way too large.

4.17   **Percentages of Items Judged to Be Linked to Inherited Academic Aptitudes**

Subject	% Inherited Academic Aptitude Items
Reading	40%
Language Arts	35%
Mathematics	20%
Science	55%
Social Studies	50%

Reason 3: Noninstructional Factors

In Chapter 3, you learned that the first two major reasons standardized achievement tests ought not be used to evaluate the quality of students' schooling were (1) teaching/testing mismatches and (2) the elimination of important, teacher-emphasized content in the quest for score-spread. Now it's time for the formal statement of Reason 3:

Standardized achievement tests should not be used to judge the quality of students' schooling because factors other than instruction also influence students' performance on these tests.

I hope you understand why I decided to treat this third reason in a chapter all by itself. You needed to see and analyze the sorts of items that abound in current standardized achievement tests. Knowing what's out there, how can we say that students' scores on these tests are directly attributable to the quality of teachers' instructional efforts? The test scores might reflect what was taught, *or* students' socioeconomic status, *or* students' inherited academic aptitudes, *or* some combination of these three factors. We can attribute an observed instructional effect to any of these causes. How sensible is it to focus on only one?

The task before educators is to provide pivotal policymakers with the information they need to disabuse themselves of the erroneous idea that it's possible to ascertain the caliber of schooling from students' scores on standardized achievement tests. Eradicating the ignorance is the key to eliminating ignorance-based errors. It is wrong to evaluate schools based on students' standardized achievement test scores. Educators and noneducators alike need to understand why.

Creating Large-Scale Tests That Illuminate Instructional Decisions

5

HAVING DISCUSSED AT SOME LENGTH THE DEEPLY-SEATED PROBLEMS AND damaging consequences of improperly constructed large-scale tests, I want to switch gears and talk about *properly constructed tests*: those that significantly illuminate the instructional decisions a teacher must make. In this chapter, I'll explain how to build a state-level accountability test that will help teachers make better instructional decisions and thus help kids learn better. I'll talk about how to analyze the quality of any large-scale standardized achievement test—national, state, or even district level. I'll also provide an example of the kind of *instructionally illuminating* assessment I have in mind.

I want to begin by saying there is an awful lot I could tell you about test development. I am, in fact, a *recovering test developer*. For many years, I headed a group that built high-stakes tests for more than a dozen states, and I made my share of misery-inducing mistakes while trying to create large-scale assessments that might help teachers teach better. I've drawn upon these hard-won and painfully derived insights to come up with this chapter's four rules, neatly listed in Figure 5.1.

5.1 Four Rules for Creating an Instructionally Illuminating Large-Scale Assessment

---

1. Identify the most important student outcomes and then develop tests for a few high priority outcomes that can be successfully taught and accurately assessed in the time available.

2. Construct all assessment tasks so an appropriate response will typically require the student to employ (1) key enabling knowledge or subskills, (2) the evaluative criteria that will be used to judge a response's quality, or (3) both of these.

3. Create a companion assessment description that spells out for teachers the essence of what's being measured by the test's items or tasks.

4. Review the items and description(s) of any high-stakes test at a level of rigor commensurate with the intended uses of the test.

These rules are intended primarily for the test development staff of an agency commissioned to build a test for a high-stakes accountability system. I realize that most busy classroom teachers won't have the time to grind out the sort of test I discuss in this chapter. However, there are some elements of these rules that are quite relevant to a teacher's creation of classroom assessments. I'll sort out those elements in the next chapter, when I focus on classroom assessments and provide tips on how teachers can get more instructional mileage out of the tests they crank out themselves.

What I really want you to learn from this chapter is what a properly constructed large-scale test generally looks like—properly constructed, that is, for purposes of providing suitable instructional targets as well as accountability evidence. It's not my intention to turn you into a *developer* of such tests, but I'd like you to get a reasonable idea of how these sorts of tests are built. You'll then be in a position to lobby for their creation. They're badly needed. Now let's get down to business.

~ Rule 1 ~

Identify the most important student outcomes and then develop tests for a few high priority outcomes that can be successfully taught and accurately assessed in the time available.

The probability that successful instruction will actually take place must concern the developer of an accountability-focused large-scale test from the very outset of the test-building process. These tests are built to measure mastery of chosen content standards—the collection of knowledge and skills a state or a district has decided it wants students to acquire within a particular subject area. Deliberations about content standards take place nationally (sponsored by national subject-specialty associations) and at the state or district level. Typically, content standards are identified by designated group of teachers and curriculum experts.

My first rule for creating instructionally illuminating large-scale tests is intended to counter the subject-matter curriculum specialists' tendency toward rampant "wish listing" while they are creating the content standards these tests are built on. Because these folks know their subject inside out, they tend to cite as content standards just about everything in their field. Each of these content standards, we are told, is absolutely critical to a child's future.

For example, here in Hawaii, back in 1994, the state department of education published a set of state-sanctioned content standards containing *hundreds* of standards for public school teachers to teach. In language arts and science, respectively, there were 495 and 418 standards. There were 199 standards in mathematics and 133 in social studies. In all, there were 1,544 content standards that subject-matter specialists wanted the children of Hawaii to master.

I'm not knocking the curriculum enthusiasts who came up with this staggering number of standards, or any other standards development team for that matter. Naturally, these folks want children to master all the nifty things they themselves love about their chosen subject, whether it's language arts or history or math. And they'd like to make sure that students really do master these things by having such mastery assessed. But here's the reality: Many of the content standards on most of these wish lists will rarely be *taught*, much less *measured*. There are simply too many standards and too many bodies of knowledge vying for the limited space available on large-scale tests and in teachers' crowded lesson plans.

Think about the mind-boggling instructional expectations Hawaii's 1994 content standards placed on classroom teachers. A 4th grade teacher, for instance, was expected to promote students' mastery of nearly 120 standards in language arts alone. Instructional insanity aside, can you see how thoroughly impossible it would be to try to test students' mastery of so many standards? We'd need to test these 4th graders around-the-clock until the tykes had become teenagers! From both an assessment and an instructional perspective, too many curricular targets turn out to be no targets at all.

The simple truth is, it's impossible to assess properly all the good things we want kids to learn. Rule 1 provides a practical solution. It tells test developers to build large-scale tests that measure only the most important student outcomes that can be successfully taught within the time available for teaching and accurately assessed within the time available for testing.

The Most Important Student Outcomes

Aside from the obvious point that we most want students to learn what they most *need* to learn, there's an additional practical reason to focus high-stakes assessments on only the most important, the most *genuinely significant* student outcomes. Because accountability tests are typically installed to let both policymakers and the public know whether schools are succeeding, our aim should be to assess outcomes of such obvious worth that onlookers will regard students' mastery as a clearly commendable instructional accomplishment. When stakes are high, we just can't afford to be testing insignificant outcomes.

Part of the burden of Rule 1 falls on state boards of education, usually the party in charge of sanctioning content standards and delivering them to test developers. It is the state board of education's responsibility to ensure that the folks who determine content standards reign in their wish-listing and prioritize the knowledge and skills they want children to be taught.

To illustrate how the prioritizing process might work, suppose the officials of a state department of education have assembled a committee of 35 curriculum specialists and classroom teachers who will identify the important knowledge and significant cognitive skills the state's children should master in language arts. Let's assume that after much deliberation the committee has identified 65 content standards.

As a requisite step before these standards are passed on to the test development company for high-stakes assessment construction, state officials should require the committee to divide these 65 "important" outcomes into three groups: *essential, highly desirable,* and *desirable.* Let's assume that after extended deliberation, the committee has designated 22 content standards as essential. At this level of the importance-hierarchy, these outcomes will almost certainly consist of complex, high-level cognitive skills. Now, as painful as it certainly will be, the committee must use consensus-seeking procedures (some form of committee member balloting perhaps, or the adroit application of an electrified cattle prod) to rank the 22 essential content standards from "most important" to "least important."

After the state has delivered a set of clearly written, ranked, essential outcomes to the test development company, the test developers should begin the process of building a test to measure the highest-ranked outcomes, starting with the top-ranked one. The challenge is to devise assessments for as many of the highly ranked outcomes as possible, bearing in mind that each standard must pass muster with respect to both *teachability* and *assessment accuracy.*

Teachability

Large-scale, high-stakes tests should assess only those most important student outcomes that an average teacher can teach with reasonable success. This focus on the likelihood of successful instruction, otherwise known as "teachability," must guide the test developer's decisions about both the *nature of* and the *number of* essential content standards to include on the test. Attention to teachability, for example, will reveal those content standards that turn out to be tapping a student's inherited intellectual aptitude rather than any skill that a teacher can promote in a classroom. The key question for test developers is, "Can this potentially assessable content standard actually be taught by most teachers, using non-Herculean instructional approaches, in the teaching time that's available to them?" In other words, we must require test developers to *think instructionally.*

Back in the 1960s and '70s, educators and test developers both learned an important lesson from the widespread advocacy of behavioral objectives. As some of you may remember, by framing instructional objectives into hundreds of small-scope, albeit well explicated, instructional aims, the advocates of behavioral objectives ended up overwhelming teachers with too many instructional targets. As a result, most teachers paid little attention to the endless lists of crisply stated but often trifling behavioral objectives. Similarly, if the assessment targets of high-stakes tests are going to function as an instructional focus for teachers, then it is imperative that only a teachable number of a field's content standards be designated for high-stakes assessment. In my experience, a half-dozen or so assessment targets make much more sense than a dozen or more.

Fortunately, it is usually possible to conceptualize content standards (even those that are stated too broadly or too vaguely) so that typical teachers can successfully promote mastery. Consider the following set of 4th grade "listening skills" from Hawaii's 1994 language arts content standards:

- Apply strategies of active, critical listening.
- Identify speaker's purpose.
- Set own purposes for listening.

• Follow a sequence of orally presented information.
• Identify main ideas and supporting details.
• Listen without being distracted.
• Evaluate information and assess validity.
• Identify implied meanings when listening to an oral presentation (Hawaii State Commission on Performance Standards, 1994, p. 18).

As a teacher, how would you go about promoting mastery of this litany of small skills? Realistically, how would you promote the skill of "listening without being distracted"? Given the eight listening skills listed above, assessment and curriculum folks—working together and following the guidelines of Rule 1—might come up with a single, more comprehensive skill that also provides teachers with a clearer instructional target. They might phrase it something like this:

> After hearing an in-person or recorded oral presentation of reasonable length, students will subsequently be able to respond accurately to written questions regarding the presentation's main features and, within reason, its subtleties.

This outcome is clear enough and intellectually specific enough to be taught and tested in a classroom. It gives teachers a pretty solid idea about what the students should really be able to do. Plus, it's important—this is definitely a skill we'd like children to acquire. But it's still to be determined if this outcome is *important enough* to secure a pricey piece of real estate on a high-stakes, large-scale test.

I want to note that subsuming lesser subskills into more significant and comprehensive ones will not eliminate the need to rank all content standards. There will almost always still be too many comprehensive skills to test properly. But the ranking of content standards will be far more manageable for those who must do it.

Accurate Assessment

The second consideration for test developers deciding which of the most important student outcomes to assess on the high-stakes test is whether those outcomes can be accurately assessed within the time available for testing. There are two critical questions to answer. First, for each content standard, test developers must ask themselves, "What is the minimum number of test items I need to devote to this content standard to support a valid inference about a student's mastery?" Second, test developers must consider the minimum number of items they need per-standard in light of the maximum number of items the test's time frame will allow. In other words, they need to ask a question akin to, "If I need an average of five items per standard, how many outcomes can I reasonably address within a test that students must complete within 90 minutes?"

As we all recall from Chapter 2, test results that do not support valid inferences about students' mastery of the assessed content are instructionally useless. If students' scores on high-stakes tests are to be the basis for programs of educational reform, these tests must include a sufficient numbers of items for each content standard to provide a measure of students' *per-standard* mastery. Teachers must be able to see how students did on specific outcomes so that they can tailor their instruction appropriately.

Let's take a look at the ugly alternative. Say you're a middle school social studies teacher and your state's officials use a large-scale test that claims to measure 75 content standards in social studies. Each year, you receive an overall report that gives your students' "percentage of content-standards mastery." To your distress, for the past few years, your school's students haven't done all that well on the state test's social studies section. You'd like your students to do better. But you simply don't know which social studies content standards they're doing badly on and which they're actually mastering. You can't design improved instructional procedures if you don't know what improvements you need to make!

Because an instructionally illuminating large scale test will provide per-standard mastery rate information, test developers will need to devote a number of test items to the assessment of each particular content standard. Given the time limitations of test administration, what this means is that in some instances, the high-stakes test may only assess a small proportion of the content standards originally identified—perhaps the top five content standards ranked as "essential," rather than the eight originally submitted. However, having insisted on the refining and prioritizing of curricular outcomes, we can be sure that the most important content standards are most likely to make the cut and to be accurately assessed.

With all my talk about limiting the number of outcomes measured on large-scale tests, I want to stress that educators are not prevented from teaching students *all* the wonderful things that ought to be taught simply because only the highest-priority content standards are being assessed by an accountability-focused test. The entire original array of content standards that state curriculum teams generate will still be eligible for *instruction*. Provided teachers have time to do so, they can and should still pursue all essential, highly desirable, and desirable curricular outcomes and assess students' mastery through in-class observations or classroom tests.

A Caution About "Counterfeit Coalescence"

I've treated Rule 1 in a fair amount of detail because if it isn't followed, the rest of the rules don't make any difference. Far too many high-stakes test development efforts are educationally doomed from the outset because they've had to start from a lengthy laundry list of vague content standards.

Because my purpose is to clarify the features of what is and what is not a properly constructed large-scale, high-stakes test, I want to caution you about a supposed solution strategy that might appear to solve the problem Rule 1 addresses, but doesn't. In response to well-warranted criticisms of "wish-list" content standards, some curriculum specialists have reduced their state's content standards to a more reasonable number of broader standards. Then they have further exemplified what each of these broader standards actually means by listing a set of "benchmarks," "indicators," or some similar descriptor that spells out in more precise terms what students should be taught to do to master each broadened content standard. Unfortunately, closer scrutiny of these efforts usually reveals that there has been no coalescing at all. Teachers and testers still have to focus on the same lengthy litanies of instructional outcomes—the only difference is that these outcomes now nestle happily under a set of new labels such as "performance indicators."

In Florida, for example, there are only six 9th and 10th grade mathematics benchmarks identified for assessment via a statewide mathematics test. But take a look at the following benchmark—one of those six—and notice how chock-full of content it actually is:

> The student uses concrete and graphic models to derive formulas for finding perimeter, area, surface area, circumference, and volume of two- and three-dimensional shapes, including rectangular solids, cylinders, cones, and pyramids (Florida Department of Education, 2001, p. 5B).

Sharp-eyed folks like you can see that this "single target" is positively crammed with different things for kids to do. The math mavens in Florida, like lots of other state curriculum committees, *appear* to be providing teachers (and testers) with a more limited set of targets, but each of those targets is bulging! There are too many things going on in such bulging benchmarks for teachers (or students) to keep track of.

This "counterfeit coalescence" isn't the answer. Content standards for instructionally illuminating tests should be few in number, but as significant, clear, testable, and teachable as possible. Now let's move on to Rule 2, which delves deeper into how test developers can support teachers' instructional efforts and, ultimately, students' learning.

~ Rule 2 ~
Construct all assessment tasks so an appropriate response will typically require the student to employ (1) key enabling knowledge or subskills, (2) the evaluative criteria that will be used to judge a response's quality, or (3) both of these.

The second rule deals with the tasks or *items* that make up large-scale tests. There are two essential types of assessment tasks: those that elicit some sort of *selected response* (such as a multiple-choice item) and those that elicit some sort of *constructed response* (such as a short answer, essay response, or oral report).

Perhaps it will prove useful to explain briefly how it is that test developers usually go about generating test items. I've created more than my share over the years (and have probably experienced at least some cerebral damage from doing so). I'll try to sketch the process without lapsing into too much rarified *psychometric* jargon.

The first thing an item-writer considers is the nature of the cognitive demand inherent in a specific content standard. What intellectual operations does the student need to carry out in order to display mastery of that content standard? What must go on inside a student's skull for an item's correct answer to bubble forth? A third way of asking this question is, "What must a student know or be able to do?" This question, in all its forms, seeks to identify the enabling knowledge and subskills a student must have in order to achieve the content standard's specified outcome.

As an example, one of the 4th grade science content standards measured on Virginia's statewide assessment reads, "The student will investigate and understand basic plant anatomy and life processes," (Commonwealth of Virginia Board of Education, 1995, p. 4). The implied cognitive demands (highly simplified here for the purposes of illustration) are for students to (1) recall, from memory, the correct names of various parts of plants, (2) recall what each part does, and (3) understand how those parts function together to sustain plant life.

After isolating a content standard's implied cognitive demands through the fiendishly complicated and time-consuming process of *task analysis* (which begins with the specified outcome and works backward, identifying any earlier knowledge and skills that students must posses before they would be able to accomplish the task beyond it), the item-writer considers eligible subject matter that might elicit those cognitive demands from test-takers. In this example, an item-writer could focus test items on roots, stems, leaves, the various parts of the flower, and processes like photosynthesis, respiration, and pollination.

The next step is to select a task type. Both selected response and constructed response items would be appropriate for this 4th grade science standard. A multiple-choice item might ask students to identify which of four plant parts listed is the site of chlorophyll production; an essay-type constructed response question might ask students to explain the role stamens and pistils play in pollination. Although the item-types are different, in each example, the cognitive demand placed on students is an appropriate one.

Having identified the standard's cognitive demands and decided on the item content and task-types, your standard item-writer would then move on to other issues, such as the number of items to use for each standard. What I'm saying in Rule 2 is that item-writers need to linger a little longer over the design of their assessment tasks. Item design is an altogether too often overlooked opportunity to support classroom instruction activities. The task analysis process item-writers engage in puts them in a wonderful position to help teachers figure out how an assessed content standard might be *taught*.

The question test developers must answer is, "How can I build a test that will help teachers *promote* the content standard(s) being measured?" Rule 2 lays it out: Item-writers must deliberately incorporate into each test item (selected response and constructed response) any necessary knowledge and subskills students must know—and must be taught—if students are to master the content standard being assessed. For constructed response items, item-writers must also work in any evaluative criteria that will be used to judge the quality of students' responses.

Key Enabling Knowledge and Subskills

The rationale for explicitly calling for students to use the complete array of enabling knowledge and subskills that task mastery requires is obvious: If students need to master subskills *X*, *Y*, and *Z* as well as knowledge *Q* in order to attain a target instructional objective, teachers need to *know* this so they can *teach* subskills *X*, *Y*, and *Z* and knowledge *Q*. By building test items that specifically call out each of the components necessary for mastery, the test developer can sensitize teachers to what's instructionally important.

Thanks to Rule 1, the developers of instructionally illuminating large-scale high-stakes tests will begin their item-building activities with a small number of content standards, almost all of them complex, high-level cognitive skills. Naturally, the higher a standard's cognitive level, the more complex and more numerous its implicit cognitive demands will be—and the more knowledge and skills a child will need to use in order to satisfy those demands.

Let's say that an instructionally skilled test developer is trying to build a test to measure a student's ability to *write a persuasive essay about a current controversial political issue.* To demonstrate mastery of this high-level cognitive outcome, students would have to recall knowledge about the political issue (including various facts, figures, supporting and opposing viewpoints) and apply that knowledge in their essay responses by choosing those facts that best support the positions they are taking. This task's cognitive demands further require students to employ the considerable ensemble of subskills necessary to create a well-written persuasive essay. These would include not only fairly general subskills such as the mechanics of forming sentences and paragraphs and the use of grammar, but also some skills that are specific to writing persuasive essays— for example, the ability to foresee an opposing argument and deal with it practically.

Evaluative Criteria

Rule 2 also says that if there are particular evaluative criteria (set forth in a rubric) that will be used to determine if a student's response to a constructed response item is acceptable, then teachers need to know that those evaluative criteria will be playing a significant role in determining the adequacy of a student's response. For instance, the persuasive essay on a controversial political topic might need to incorporate *appropriate mechanics* (spelling, punctuation, grammar), *suitable content, skillful organization*, and one or more effective *persuasion strategies.* A scoring rubric for judging students' responses would probably incorporate those same four evaluative criteria.

As this example illustrates, more often than not, a scoring rubric's evaluative criteria will be similar, if not identical, to the key enabling knowledge/subskills identified during any reasonable task analysis. Obviously, teachers must teach their students to recognize and understand those evaluative criteria well enough to be able to engage in meaningful self-evaluation of their own efforts.

The Instructional Pay-Off

A test developer who "thinks instructionally" will make sure that all the enabling knowledge and subskills or evaluative criteria incorporated into assessment tasks can be taught. The test developer then must decide whether a typical teacher, using any sort of reasonable teaching approach, could provide students with the instruction they'll need to master this set of enabling knowledge and subskills. Again, as Rule 1 indicated, instructionally illuminating tests should not require an atypically splendid teacher.

When the task analysis of this content standard is complete, a test developer who follows Rule 2 will create a variety of test items that are appropriate measures of a student's ability to master the learning outcome being assessed. At the end of this chapter, I include several additional examples of what test items on an instructionally illuminating assessment might look like.

I want to close the discussion of Rule 2 by pointing out that the kind of instructionally illuminating assessment I'm talking about will *not* require teachers to use any particular form of instruction to promote student learning. Experience indicates that for most curricular outcomes, there are many roads to instructional Mecca. Yet, no matter *how* a teacher provides instruction, the test developer's careful analysis of a content standard and teaching-focused task construction can support the instructional process by revealing the things students really must learn before they can master the important outcomes assessed on large-scale tests. Rule 3 goes further in this direction.

~ Rule 3 ~

Create a companion assessment description that spells out for teachers the essence of what's being measured by the test's items or tasks.

Even with a carefully designed, instructionally illuminating test, many teachers will need assistance determining exactly what the critical instructional elements of the content standard are. Rule 3 requires test developers to eliminate as much mystery as possible by providing an *assessment description* for each content standard measured on the high-stakes, large-scale test.

Assessment descriptions are tools for teachers—short documents that delineate as clearly as possible the important features of each content standard being assessed and present the information both succinctly and at a level of detail sufficient to help teachers make on-target instructional plans. Rule 3 is about clarity. Its rationale: The better teachers understand the nature of the assessed content standard, the more effective they'll be at promoting students' mastery of that content standard. Simply put, it's easier—and smarter—to teach toward clear targets than toward murky ones.

The Well-Written Assessment Description

At the close of this chapter, I devote several pages to a sample assessment description and everything that should accompany it. What I want to do here is give you a framework for what an assessment description should contain so that when you come to my sample (or to any real-life assessment description), you'll know the features to look for.

Given the considerable variety in the nature of content standards to be assessed (and the range of enabling knowledge or subskills associated with each one), there's no single assessment description template that will always work satisfactorily in all classroom settings. The two chief attributes of a well-written assessment description are (1) it accurately isolates the enabling knowledge or subskills and evaluation criteria required for task mastery and (2) it does so concisely. For example, an assessment description for *Intellectual Skill X* might spell out that mastery depends on

- Body of Knowledge A.
- Body of Knowledge B.
- The subskill to apply Knowledge A and Knowledge B so that previously unencountered phenomena can be classified as either C or D.
- The subskill to use Evaluative Criteria 1, 2, and 3 to determine if any given C is better than any given D.

The enabling knowledge and subskills identified in the assessment description should be limited to what is *distinctively* necessary for a student's mastery of the content standard being assessed. For example, if high school students need to be able to read reasonably well to pass a printed social studies test, it would not be necessary to isolate "reading" as an enabling subskill. Clearly, if a social studies teacher were to discover that some students are nonreaders, the teacher would need to tackle this important deficit instructionally; however, basic enabling subskills like reading and writing need not be spelled out in an assessment description.

Knowledge-Specific Supplements

When teachers need to promote students' mastery of a body of factual knowledge (whether the knowledge is an enabler for a content standard or is the content standard itself), teachers must be able to teach the *entire* set of knowledge. Even if the actual test requires students to be familiar with only a *sample* of that knowledge, the assessment description must provide the complete set of information, facts, and rules that students should be taught to master. Teachers should not be forced to guess what knowledge they must transfer to their students.

The most efficient way for test developers to alert teachers to large sets of knowledge is to provide a separate supplement to the assessment description. For example, if an important cognitive skill in science requires students to have mastered an enabling vocabulary of 90 scientific terms, then all 90 terms should be identified in a description supplement. If this vocabulary is particularly important enabling knowledge, the supplement should be structured in a way that helps teachers plan instructional activities to promote students' mastery of all 90 terms. If the content standard being assessed deals exclusively with a set of information to be memorized, then this information—in its entirety—must be explicitly provided to teachers so they can teach it to their students.

Illustrative Sample Items

The assessment description should also be accompanied by a modest number of varied and nonexhaustive sample items to help teachers understand what sorts of test items their students will be facing when the high-stakes test is administered. These items should be as varied in format as possible, with both selected response items and constructed response items (written and oral). Every one of the sample items provided should contribute to a valid mastery of the content standard being assessed. However, the samples must be clearly identified as nonexhaustive. Teachers referencing these sample items need to be aware that these are not necessarily the items students will face on the actual test.

I've been pretty clear on what I think of the practice of teaching to tests. As educators, our objective is to promote students' *generalizable* mastery of a designated set of knowledge or skills, not their ability to respond to a particular type of test item. By making it clear that students will need to be able to apply the identified skills and knowledge in a variety of formats, the test developer can encourage teachers to teach in a way that will help students demonstrate their mastery in a variety of ways. To truly promote student *learning*, teachers must focus instruction on the content standard's cognitive demand.

To sum up Rule 3, test developers should provide teachers with assessment descriptions and supplements for each content standard assessed on large-scale, high stakes tests. These documents, built to reflect what's being measured and spelled out in teacher-palatable language focused on the test's cognitive demands, are the chief way that these properly constructed tests can actually contribute to successful instructional decision making.

~ Rule 4 ~

Review the items and description(s) of any high-stakes test at a level of rigor commensurate with the test's intended uses.

Anybody who has anything to do with education knows it's wise to always double-check one's work. How would test developers go about confirming that a large-scale accountability test created in accordance with Rules 1 through 3 will actually function as it was intended? They would review the test itself.

Rule 4 rule says that the more important the test, the more exacting should be the review of that test's items and its assessment descriptions. I'm not saying that classroom teachers shouldn't carefully review the instructionally illuminating tests they create themselves. But the review methods I advocate as the best way to confirm that a test has been properly constructed would be a load of work for a busy teacher. I honestly can't think of very many psychologically sound teachers willing to take this on as a routine part of their job.

I'm focusing here on the review procedures for the really high-stakes tests, such as those that might determine grade-to-grade promotion or diploma denial. These are the tests with assessment missions deemed so significant that meaningful financial resources will be available to support both their construction *and* an item-by-item appraisal to ensure the items have been constructed properly.

Evaluators

Who would do all this evaluating? Because the objective is to ensure that the test created will illuminate teachers' instructional decision making, most of the judges who evaluate high-stakes test should be classroom teachers with experience teaching students to master the content standards the test will assess. For a significant high-stakes test, I would recommend assembling a review panel of 15–25 individuals. A few of the panel members should be instructional specialists (for example, instructional psychology professors) and a few should be curriculum experts (for example, district office curriculum supervisors). But I'd want my review panels to consist mainly of firing-line teachers.

Evaluation Criteria

What would we ask the members of such a review panel to do? The review panel's purpose is to function as external quality monitors. As such, the members' responsibility would be to analyze the test's tasks and assessment descriptions, and determine whether the test is good enough to use in the high-stakes setting for which it is intended.

Although this chapter is not the appropriate place for a detailed, step-by-step description of how a review panel should judge a high-stakes test, I do want to suggest several criteria around which any decent review should be organized. First, attention should be given to the test's items with respect to curricular congruence, instructional sensitivity, out-of-school factors, and bias. Attention should also be given to the instructional illumination and palatability of the test's assessment descriptions. If the test measures multiple content standards, it would be important to make sure that the collection of assessment descriptions *in aggregate* is not too overwhelming for teachers.

Each member of the review panel should be prepared to answer one or more questions related to each of these evaluative dimensions. Panelists might respond in a binary fashion—for example, *Yes* or *No*—or perhaps by using some sort of multipoint scale. If desired, an *Uncertain* response option might be added to the *Yes* or *No* choices.

To illustrate the kinds of questions that could be given to panelists, I have provided one example question for each of the evaluative dimensions I cited above. Because these sorts of questions need to be carefully crafted for the specific high-stakes test under review, the following are intended to be only illustrative.

Here are some sample questions related to tasks or test items:
- *Curricular Congruence.* Would a student's response to this item, along with others, contribute to a valid determination of whether the student has mastered the specific content standard the item is supposed to be measuring?
- *Instructional Sensitivity.* If a teacher is, with reasonable effectiveness, attempting to promote students' mastery of the content standard that this item is supposed to measure, is it likely that most of the teacher's students will be able to answer the item correctly?
- *Out-of-School Factors.* Is this item essentially free of content that would make a student's socioeconomic status or inherited academic aptitudes the dominant influence on how the student will respond?

- *Bias*. Is this item free of content that might offend or unfairly penalize students because of personal characteristics such as race, gender, ethnicity, or socioeconomic status?

Here are sample questions related to assessment descriptions:

- *Instructional Illumination*. After reading this assessment description, would a teacher have a clear idea about the cognitive demands placed on students, so that the teacher could plan effective instruction to have students master the content standard being measured?

- *Palatability*. Is this assessment description sufficiently understandable and concise so that a teacher would be willing to read it carefully?

If review panels have been carefully selected, and panelists have been properly oriented to their review tasks, the resultant judgmental evidence regarding the test's items and its assessment description should be adequate to determine whether the test is indeed an instructionally illuminating test suitable for use in the specific high-stakes setting for which it was created. As noted earlier, I'd probably also want to ask the review panel if the complete set of assessment descriptions was too lengthy to be used by busy teachers.

A Caveat About Teacher Support

Now that you've read my four rules and the reasons for them, I need to make an important point. Merely creating instructionally illuminating tests will *not* automatically lead to improved instruction because a good many teachers will not know how to make use of such tests and the clarity they provide. Very few teachers, for example, have been trained to read a succinct description of an assessed content standard and then plan their instruction accordingly.

Let's assume that teachers are going to be spurred by a nontraditional, instructionally oriented large-scale assessment program to pursue a small number of significant cognitive skills. If that's so, then many of those teachers will need help learning how to promote student mastery of such skills. Pursuit of these complex and demanding skills will call for a truly different approach to instruction.

For this reason, when an instructionally illuminating high-stakes test is made available to teachers, it should be accompanied by a variety of suggested teaching strategies that teachers might consider using. In other words, because many teachers will not know how to take advantage of instructionally illuminating tests, we must help them do so. This help could take the form of general or specific ideas about how to instruct students in a manner that will facilitate mastery of the assessed content standard. Teachers would be free to consider these suggestions, adopt some, or adopt none; it would be the teacher's choice. In any event, there would have been a meaningful attempt to help teachers capitalize on the opportunities to deliver better instruction brought about by the availability of instructionally illuminating tests.

A Sample Assessment Description and Test Items

I want to close this chapter with Figure 5.2's example of a complete assessment description and sample test items for an instructionally illuminating test. Remember: Effective assessment descriptions will provide teachers with a sufficiently clear idea about the content standard being measured to enable them to provide instruction targeted to the knowledge and skills described.

The demanding nature of the skill I present in this sample exemplifies the approach I'm recommending for large-scale assessment. With only a small number of outcomes to be assessed by large-scale testing programs, every one of them needs be powerful and demanding, such as students' ability to write expository essays or, as in this case, their ability to use history's lessons to analyze current-day problems. To quote a parent who recently looked over this assessment description, "If my kids could actually do this, it would knock my socks off!" If we could demonstrate that students have, over time, increased their mastery of this high-powered skill, both parents and policymakers should readily concede that some first-rate learning has taken place. And first-rate learning, of course, is heavily dependent on first-rate teaching.

I don't pretend that the sample assessment description you're about to see constitutes the "final word," or that it couldn't be improved by teachers who have more experience than I do in teaching the content involved. But I hope it will give you an idea of the sort of descriptive scheme I have in mind. At the conclusion of this illustrative assessment description, I'd like to draw your attention to several of its most important features, then show you how such assessment descriptions can play a pivotal role in helping teachers design more effective instruction. A final note: The idea to assess this kind of high-level skill in history occurred to me during my recent work with educators from the Department of Defense Dependents School in Hessen, Germany. I appreciate their insights.

Analyzing the Sample Assessment Description

Let's look closer at this illustrative assessment description to see what it's doing. First, please note that it's fairly brief. Be wary of lengthy assessment descriptions. They tend to be more completely accurate, but they also tend to be off-putting to the would-be reader. Busy teachers rarely have the patience to struggle through a multi-page document.

In the first section of this assessment description, we learn that a student is going to be given "a prose account of a real or fictitious problem, as well as a proposed solution to that problem." The teacher now knows exactly what the students are going to be facing. Then the description delineates the four subtasks that—separately or in combination—the student must be able to perform. Given a problem and a proposed solution to it, the student must be able to (1) *identify* a relevant historical event(s), (2) *justify* the event's relevance, (3) *predict* the proposed solution's consequences, and (4) *support* that prediction. The teacher should now be clear on the nature of the eligible cognitive demands any of the assessment items might place on students. And that clarity will contribute to the teacher's isolation of any pertinent enabling subskills or bodies of knowledge. These, of course, would also need to be taught to the student.

The assessment description's second section spells out the assessment possibilities for the four subtasks. Students may be required to respond to a "mix and match" of subtasks or to all four

5.2 A Sample Assessment Description: "Using History's Lessons"

Introduction. This assessment description and the illustrative tasks that follow it are intended for use by 11th and 12th graders taking a U.S. history course. The skill could be promoted at earlier grade levels, with both the language and the task's cognitive complexity simplified. Before attempting to measure this skill, consult the appropriate state or district curriculum standards to identify the eligible historical events for students to consider. As an example, the following historical events were identified as suitable by one large school district for its 11th and 12th grade U.S. history courses:

The Constitution	The New Deal
Territorial Expansion	World War II
The Civil War	The Cold War
Reconstruction	The Korean "Police Action"
The Industrial Revolution	The Civil Rights Movement
Imperialism	The Vietnam War
The Spanish American War	The Communication Revolution
World War I	The Depression

Assessment Task. Given a prose account of a real or fictitious current problem, as well as a proposed solution to that problem, students will be able to respond appropriately to any one or any combination of the following subtasks:

Subtask 1. Identify at least one significant historical event (such as The Industrial Revolution) that is, at least in part, germane to the problem and its proposed solution.

Subtask 2. Justify the relevance of the identified historical event(s) to the problem and its proposed solution.

Subtask 3. Make a defensible history-based prediction regarding the proposed solution's likely consequences.

Subtask 4. Support that prediction on the basis of parallels between the identified historical event(s) and the proposed problem-solution.

Although the assessment may ask students to supply responses to individual subtasks so that their mastery of those particular types of subtasks can be determined, it will ultimately require all students to respond to a comprehensive task such as the one immediately following the Sample Problem Situation and Proposed Solution. Please note: When the assessment asks students to respond to a comprehensive task, it will provide a *different* problem and proposed solution than those used for measuring mastery of individual subtasks.

5.2 A Sample Assessment Description: "Using History's Lessons"—*continued*

A Sample Problem Situation and Proposed Solution

Directions: Read the problem described and the proposed solution to that problem, then respond to the task (or tasks) provided.

WAR OR PEACE

Nation A is a large, industrialized country with a population nearing 100,000,000. Nation A has ample resources, and is democratically governed. Nation A also owns two groups of islands that, although distant, are rich in iron ore and petroleum.

Nation B is a country with far fewer natural resources and a population of only 40,000,000. In terms of land mass, Nation B is about one-third as large as Nation A. Although much less industrialized than Nation A, Nation B is as technologically advanced as Nation A. Nation B is governed by a three-member council of generals.

Recently, without any advance warning, Nation B's military forces attacked Nation A. As a consequence of this attack, more than half of Nation A's military equipment was destroyed, leaving it with fewer military resources than Nation B. After Nation B's highly successful surprise attack, its leaders issued "peace terms" calling for Nation A to turn over its two groups of islands to Nation B. Nation B's leaders also announced that if Nation A does not concede these islands, Nation B will engage Nation A in an all-out war.

Nation A's elected leaders are now faced with a choice between (1) peace obtained by giving up the islands or (2) war with a militarily stronger nation. Nation A's leaders decide to declare that a state of war exists with Nation B. They believe that even though Nation B currently has greater military strength, in the long term Nation A will prevail because of its greater industrial capability and richer natural resources.

Sample Comprehensive Task. In an essay, drawing on your knowledge of U.S. history, (1) Select one or more important historical events that are especially relevant to the fictitious situation described above; (2) Justify the relevance of your selection(s); (3) Make a reasonable history-based prediction about the likely consequences of the decision by Nation A's leaders to go to war; (4) Defend your prediction on the basis of the historical event(s) you identified.

Note on Evaluative Criteria: The evaluation of a student's response to this four-step, comprehensive task will be based on the quality with which each of the following have been carried out: [1] event(s) selection, [2] event(s) justification, [3] history-based prediction, and [4] defense of prediction.

5.2 A Sample Assessment Description: "Using History's Lessons"—*continued*

Sample Items for Measuring Subtask Mastery. Sample items keyed to specific subtasks are listed below.

Sample Item for Subtask 1. The "War and Peace" problem description discusses two fictitious nations. From the four choices below, choose the two nations and the armed conflict *most* comparable to those described.

A.	<u>Conflict:</u>	World War I
	<u>Nations:</u>	U.S. and Italy
B.	<u>Conflict:</u>	Korean "Police Action"
	<u>Nations:</u>	U.S. and North Korea
C.	<u>Conflict:</u>	The Spanish American War
	<u>Nations:</u>	U.S. and Spain
D.	<u>Conflict:</u>	World War II
	<u>Nations:</u>	U.S. and Japan

Sample Item for Subtask 2. In an oral presentation of one-to-two minutes duration, identify at least one important historical event that is especially pertinent to the problem situation described, then justify why you believe this to be so.

Sample Item for Subtask 3. The final paragraph of the "War and Peace" problem description identifies two proposed solutions: (1) peace obtained at the cost of giving up the two groups of islands or (2) going to war against a militarily stronger nation. Relying on your knowledge of U.S. history, please choose *one* of those two proposed solutions, then predict what is likely to happen if that choice is made.

_____

_____

_____

_____

_____

_____

_____

Sample Item for Subtask 4. For the previous item you were to make a history-based prediction about a proposed solution's likely consequences. Now, using the response booklet that has been provided, please draw on parallel events in the history of the United States to defend the reasonableness of your prediction.

subtasks combined. The assessment description also makes clear that at some point, the students will be required to respond to a comprehensive task that incorporates the cognitive demands of all four subtasks.

Analyzing the Sample Tasks

The set of illustrative but nonexhaustive tasks that accompany the assessment description provide the teacher with further clarification. As you see, the test developer has provided a variety of task-types to communicate to teachers the need to promote students' *generalizable* skill-mastery, not merely mastery of one type of test item. And notice that for the sake of brevity and ease of teacher reading, all four of the illustrative subtasks have been based on the same sample problem and proposed solution. (If other sorts of test items were to be used for a completely different sort of skill, they would typically be set out as independent items, not dependent on the same stimulus material.)

Analyzing the Instructional Benefits

Properly written assessment descriptions can help teachers clarify the nature of the skills being sought. If those descriptions are accompanied by instructional suggestions, and if the *number* of skills is reasonably small, then the large-scale assessment can enhance the quality of instruction teachers present in their classrooms. With a clear understanding of both the target skills they should be promoting and the kind of the tasks that students might face on the test, teachers can design more effective instruction.

In this example, students must definitely become familiar with the designated, grade-appropriate historical events. But as the assessment description helps make plain, students will need to understand those historical events in a special way—beyond memorizing "names and dates." They will need to understand if there are any important *lessons* that can be drawn from each of those historical events. To promote this, teachers will need to present instruction in a way that brings such history-based lessons to the forefront. Moreover, teachers will need to stress the relevance of these lessons to current problems. Be assured, if a history teacher sets out to promote students' mastery of this powerful history-based skill, it will mark an end to "same-old, same-old" history instruction.

And that leads me re-emphasize an earlier point. The architects of nontraditional, instructionally illuminating large-scale assessment programs should support teachers' efforts by supplying a series of instructional suggestions—some with general applicability and some targeted to particular skills being assessed. For instance, in the "Using History's Lessons" skill, test developers might offer teachers *general* advice about the importance of providing students with on-target guided and independent practice, along with a solid dose of modeling and a flock of feedback. But teachers should also be given *specific* suggestions about how they might go about teaching a *particular* skill. For instance, test developers might provide a *skill-specific* task analysis—a task analysis based exclusively on this historical skill. They also might suggest that teachers incorporate into any discussion of historical events a forthright consideration of whether there are any lessons to be drawn from those events, and whether those lessons might be helpful in coping with current-day problems. Students need to be taught how to analyze historical events; if this instruction is strong, it is likely that students will become capable of judging whether given historical events do or do not provide lessons that apply to the present.

Let me stress again that teachers would not need to follow the suggestions provided. However, considering the atypicality of the teaching chore, I believe most teachers would welcome a set of skill-specific instructional ideas.

A Case Summation for Instructionally Illuminating Large-Scale Tests

I want to close this chapter by stating that the kind of nontraditional, large-scale assessments I've described and illustrated—those that (1) focus on a limited number of the most important content standards; (2) incorporate enabling knowledge and subskills; (3) are accompanied by clear, teacher-friendly assessment descriptions; and (4) are quality-checked by evaluative panels of educators—could have an extraordinarily positive effect on U.S. education. Yes, these tests would supply the accountability evidence and proof of standards-mastery so widely sought through high-stakes testing programs. But more importantly, they would help teachers teach better and, as a consequence, help students learn better. And isn't that the whole point of what we do? I hope that you will take information presented in this chapter and use it to persuade colleagues, parents, and educational policymakers that there's a better alternative to the current state of testing. The *right* kinds of high-stakes tests can both measure *and* enhance the quality of our children's education.

Getting Maximum Instructional Mileage Out of Classroom Assessment

6

IN THE LAST CHAPTER, WE COVERED FOUR RULES THAT TEST DEVELOPERS could apply to make large-scale assessments instructionally illuminating. Now it's time to focus on the classroom. As the title of this chapter suggests, what you'll find here is a collection of ideas about how teachers can use in-class tests to help make better instructional decisions and, thus, help students learn better. Figure 6.1 lists four rules focused on doing just that.

However, these rules and this chapter are *not* intended for teachers alone! The testing and teaching issues I'll be discussing lie at the very heart of education, and educators of *all* stripes really need to be familiar with them. Besides, school-site administrators and district-level administrators can do a lot to further teachers' awareness that classroom tests can be crafted with instruction in mind. The resultant tests can meaningfully improve the quality of teaching that goes on in our schools.

6.1   Four Rules for Classroom Assessment

1. Use only a modest number of major classroom tests, but make sure these tests measure learner outcomes of indisputable importance.

2. Use diverse types of classroom assessments to clarify the nature of any learning outcome you seek.

3. Make students' responses to classroom assessments central to your instructional decision making.

4. Regularly assess educationally significant student affect—but only to make inferences about groups of students, not individual students.

I've been a classroom teacher and I know how busy a teacher's life can be. Accordingly, I built this chapter's four rules for classroom assessment on two premises: *instructional contribution* and *teacher sanity*. Yes, I want teachers to use tests to support and enhance their teaching effectiveness. But I also want them maintain a modest semblance of sanity. Teachers, this chapter is intended to *help* you, not drive you crazy. I promise that you'll be able to implement these rules for more effective instruction without any need to seek extended psychotherapy.

Before we get started on my specific guidelines, there's one overarching concept, one *pre-rule rule*, if you will, that I feel I need to stress. Here it is:

Teachers, and those who work with them, should familiarize themselves with the fundamentals of classroom assessment.

No, no, don't panic! This chapter is *not* an abbreviated treatment of *everything* that teachers (and those charged with supporting teachers) should know about classroom assessment. That's a much bigger bowl of assessment soup than I would ask you to swallow in this sitting. However, to effectively follow this chapter's four rules for more instructionally illuminating classroom tests, folks really must have a basic understanding of classroom testing. Fortunately, in the last few years a number of writers have authored first-rate books that specifically address classroom assessment. I've listed several in the References and Resources section. All the books I've cited are loaded with solid information on important assessment concepts such as validity, how to avoid biased tests, what a rubric is, and what reliability isn't. These books also contain experience-honed, practical guidelines about how to build essay items that shine and multiple-choice items that sparkle.

In short, there are lots of good books out there that capture the things *all* educators (anyone who has anything to do with what goes on in a classroom) really ought to know about classroom testing. And this group certainly includes principals and assistant principals. Members of the superintendency clan could probably stand to pick up a pointer or two as well. I am not saying you must dash out and buy all the classroom assessment texts I've cited. But if you can buy or borrow just *one*, I encourage you to read it a bit at a time as your schedule permits and build your measurement moxie.

Now, proceeding on the assumption that you are conversant with the essentials of classroom assessment—or are soon to become so—let's take a look at the first of my four rules for maximizing the instructional benefits classroom assessments can provide.

~ Rule 1 ~

Use only a modest number of major classroom tests, but make sure these tests measure learning outcomes of indisputable importance.

If this first rule for making classroom assessments contribute more directly to improved instruction seems a bit familiar, that's because it closely parallels last chapter's first rule regarding large-scale assessment. Both are based on the proposition that the number of assessment targets to which a teacher can give genuine attention is far smaller than many educators assume.

Rule 1 begins by telling teachers they need not feel obliged to measure every single bit of content covered in their lesson plans. It's simply nonsensical to ask teachers to test children on everything that the teachers need to teach. Recall that in Chapter 2, I tried to convince you that educational testing was an inference-drawing enterprise. To draw valid inferences about students, we need to use tests that representatively sample an intended learning outcome. Obviously, it is better to measure a small number of learning outcomes representatively than it is to measure a larger number of outcomes unrepresentatively. If teachers' measurement methods are unsound, it will be impossible for them to make *valid* score-based inferences about student mastery from the tests' results. And *invalid* inferences about students almost always contribute to poor classroom decisions. Finally, it's just common sense that keeping a reasonable cap on the number of classroom minutes devoted to testing is an effective way to gain more time for teaching.

Rule 1's "less is more" perspective on measurement also applies to teachers' instructional emphases. In my experience, and probably yours as well, most teachers can sensibly direct their instruction toward only a modest number of instructional targets. Teachers who try to "cover the curricular waterfront" tend to end up all wet. So Rule 1 provides a little reminder that teachers can be more effective instructors when they focus on an intellectually manageable set of learning outcomes. And only the most important of these outcomes should make the testing cut.

Now I realize that teachers have many ways of figuring out if students are mastering what's being taught. Often, an insightful remark by one student or a truly dopey comment from another can send a clear signal that Student A is "getting it" and Student B is not. Besides, there are various kinds of short duration quizzes and mini-tests that teachers can use to make "dipstick" estimates of students' progress.

Rule 1 does not prohibit teachers from using these kinds of quick-and-dirty assessment techniques (or slow-and-clean ones, either). It's concerned with *major* classroom tests, such as midterm exams, final exams, and especially the tests that teachers use to tell if a lengthy unit of instruction has promoted students' mastery of significant skills. If teachers have sufficient time, energy, and sanity, they should feel free to test what they will and when they will. But if these lesser tests get in the way of measuring major learning outcomes, or divert the teacher's instructional attention from the most important learning outcomes, then Rule 1 says "Dump 'em!"

Test Content

My main advice for teachers looking to identify the targets on which to focus their assessment energy is to concentrate on cognitive skill mastery, rather than bodies of knowledge. Knowledge—that is, memorized facts, concepts, and truths of one kind or another—represents an important commodity for students to acquire. It's just that when a teacher must choose only a small number of major outcomes to measure, those outcomes probably ought not be of the knowledge-only variety.

The ability to compose a well-crafted expository essay is a good example of the kind of major outcome I'm talking about. Although essay writing requires students to recall relevant facts and information, it also requires them to demonstrate higher-level cognitive skills, such as their comprehension of that knowledge, their ability to analyze it, and their ability to effectively organize their response to communicate that understanding. Think back to the illustrative skill in U.S. history that was the subject of Chapter 5's sample assessment description. If students did not *know* a good deal about U.S. history, they'd never be able to use historical parallels to predict how the proposed "War or Peace" scenario is apt to turn out.

Teachers looking for ideas about what major outcomes to assess in class would also be wise to refer to the set of state- or district-sanctioned content standards teachers are supposed to promote. Before "content standards" were sullied by their association with accountability and large-scale testing, they were actual indicators of truly important, educationally desirable outcomes. (If properly crafted, they still are, really.) But from a purely pragmatic perspective, if the curricular authorities deem a skill sufficiently important to have been chosen as a content standard, then it makes a good deal of sense for teachers to collect classroom evidence about their students' mastery.

And, of course, that's all the more reason for curricular specialists to *prioritize* content standards so that teachers can easily identify which are the most important. If that sort of prioritizing hasn't been done, the teacher will face a laundry list of content standards—often far too many to either teach or assess. I wish I had some wonderful advice to offer to those teachers who must cope with wish-list standards, but I don't. If state or district curriculum authorities really believe that *all* of those standards should be taught, then a teacher is stuck—the absurdity of the expectation notwithstanding. The only way out is to urge curricular authorities to help teachers by carrying out at least *some* prioritizing of importance. In the meantime, teachers must continue to follow their professional judgment when it comes to determining which learning outcomes are truly significant.

Test Creation

Teachers obliged to crank out their own classroom tests will find that all of the classroom assessment texts cited in this book's References and Resources section (for example, the texts written by Airasian, McMillan, Stiggins, and yours truly) do a solid job of describing proper classroom test construction. I want to stress, though, that there is no reason all classroom teachers need to build the same classroom tests afresh, particularly if the majority of teachers are selecting major assessment targets from the same lists of district- or state-level content standards. Like wheel reinvention, test reinvention is a spectacular waste of time.

Here's an opportunity for forward-looking officials from a state department of education or a local school district to provide teachers with a set of already-constructed classroom assessment instruments designed to gauge student progress toward official content standard outcomes. If these optional assessments are sound ones, then teachers are likely to use them.

State or district officials looking to develop these instruments will often seek help from external assessment consultants. In these cases, the consultants selected definitely need to be familiar with what goes on inside a classroom and must know their instructional stuff. And I believe assessment-literate educators have a role to play in ensuring that these are the contractors entrusted with the job. (More on this in Chapter 8.)

Finally, I want to remind teachers struggling to fit new test creation into their already overcrowded schedules that they should make use of their colleagues' assessment insights. Exchanging valuable instructional material is a pretty common practice. Why not also share teacher-developed tests?

Why Important Outcomes Are So Important

Before we leave Rule 1, I want to explain my reasons for emphasizing teachers' need to measure "learning outcomes of indisputable importance" in their classroom assessment. The first reason is strictly student-rooted, and I believe we've covered it pretty thoroughly: If a teacher's assessment and instruction focus on the most important learning outcomes, then it's a decent bet the teacher's students will be learning what they most ought to be learning.

The second reason is based on educators' practical need to deliver credible evidence that schools are providing quality instruction. As we've established, there's no point in looking to current standardized achievement test scores for this kind of information. In the next chapter, we'll talk about a data-gathering approach that will yield believable evidence regarding the effectiveness of a teacher's instruction. But let me preview that discussion by asking you to make believe you're a parent whose child figures in the following assessment scenario.

Students in your child's class were asked to write persuasive essays at the start of the school year and again at its conclusion. The first set of essays were held, unevaluated, until the end of the school year. At this time, the students' beginning-of-the-year essays and their end-of-year essays were coded as such, then mixed together and passed on to a team of teachers (from another school) and parents. These nonpartisans scored each essay without knowing whether it was a written in September or in June. After all papers had been blind-scored in this manner, the secret codes were consulted, the papers were sorted into pre-instruction and post-instruction essays, and the results were compared.

Still with me? Good, because your child and your child's class have made some impressive gains. Our scenario continues with you receiving a one-page report from your child's teacher that describes the blind-scoring procedure and explains that 94 percent of the top-scored papers were written at the end of the year. And to top it off, this report is attached to a copy of your own child's pre-instruction and post-instruction persuasive essays. When you compare the two, it's clear that over the span of one school year, your child's ability to write a persuasive essay has taken a big jump in quality. In the post-instruction essay, your child's sentences are more complex, the punctuation is in place, and the thoughts are more thoroughly developed. Plus, it's far more persuasive!

Now, pretend parent, how would you react to the one-sheet data description of whole-class progress, coupled with the evidence you see for yourself in your own child's essays? I'm willing to bet that you'd be doggone pleased over your child's educational development. I certainly would! I'd conclude from this evidence that my child had been effectively taught.

Think about how much less compelling this sort of evidence would be if it dealt with a trivial outcome. For example, what if the teacher tried to do the same beginning-of-the-year/end-of-the-year comparison with a 10-item spelling quiz? Even if there were *substantial* improvement in students' scores, parents wouldn't be likely to see this as a particularly convincing indication of successful instruction.

And think again of the "Using History's Lessons" task presented with last chapter's sample assessment description. As a parent, wouldn't you be thrilled to find out that blind-scored papers indicate students in your child's class have made striking improvements in their mastery of that skill? I know of few parents (myself included) who possess the historical-interpretation skill that task measures. I have to echo the reaction of that parent friend of mine: If my kid's class could display reasonable mastery of such a high-level skill, it would knock my socks off!

So as you see, following Rule 1—focusing important classroom assessments on carefully chosen, highly significant outcomes—is in the best interest of students, who learn what they most need to know. It's in the best interest of teachers, who are able to focus their instruction to support that important learning. And it's in the best interest of educators as a whole, who gain powerful and sorely needed evidence of that learning—valuable public-relations currency in our accountability-driven environment. Let's turn now to Rule 2.

~ Rule 2 ~

Use diverse types of classroom assessments to clarify the nature of any learning outcome you seek.

Way, way back, when I was a graduate student, I learned in psychology classes about something called *operationalizing*. As my psych profs informed me, it was often necessary for researchers to deal with a variety of hidden variables, such as a person's level of anxiety, by employing previously successful problem-solution strategies. To carry out their research, those investigators had to employ some sort of *operation* that could serve as a stand-in for the unseeable.

And that's what Rule 2 deals with—the role classroom tests can play in "operationalizing" the typically *covert* cognitive skills teachers try to promote in their students. Before teachers select a state-provided classroom assessment, reuse a test designed by a colleague, or put the finishing touches on a new test they've built to incorporate a new curricular focus, they should take a good look at the test items and ask themselves this question: "What kind of cognitive operation(s) must my students engage in if they are to succeed on this test?" Another way of posing this question is, "What are the cognitive demands imposed by this test? What intellectual operation(s) does it ask students to perform?"

The cognitive demands that tests place on students are what *should* be occupying a teacher's attention and driving a teacher's instruction. Teachers who spend even a modest amount of time analyzing a test's cognitive demands will have a better idea about how to design instruction that will satisfy the requirements of a worthwhile test and promote the desired major learning outcomes.

The Dividends of Outcome Clarity

It's an overused adage, but an accurate one: *People who have a clear idea about where they're going are more likely to get there.* Let me add a corollary: *Teachers who have a clear idea of the learning outcomes their students should achieve will be more likely to help their students attain those outcomes.* Such teachers will certainly out-teach their colleagues who have only a murky notion about what their students ought to be doing when the instruction is complete.

During my more than 40 years as a dues-paying member of the education profession, I've come across many teachers who possess super-crisp concepts of what knowledge and skills they want their students to possess at instruction's end. And I've also spoken with a substantial number of classroom teachers who have only a general (and sometimes thoroughly squishy) idea about what they want their students to be able to do at the end of instruction. Rule 2 can help.

Let me toss you a concrete "let's pretend" example of how a teacher might use classroom tests to clarify a loosely defined content standard and ultimately provide students with more effective instruction. Let's pretend you're teaching an introductory high school science course, such as first-year chemistry. Among the first-year chemistry content standards approved by your state board of education is the following: *"Students will be able to interpret scientific figures, tables, and graphs."* What sorts of lessons might you plan to help your students achieve this content standard?

Well, if the content standard itself were the *only* source of your understanding about what students should be able to do when they have mastered this skill, you'd probably not have a very clear idea of the nature of the learning outcome you're seeking. My guess is that you'd conclude it was something such as, "This content standard calls for students to interpret scientific data-displays."

Based on that reasonable, very plausible interpretation of the content standard, you'd probably set out to give your students plenty of practice in trying to make sense of diverse sorts of scientific data presented in different kinds of figures, graphs, or charts. You'd spend some time explaining the key distinctions of tables, figures, and graphs, and how those distinctions might influence someone's interpretations. You might have students establish work groups to interpret different scientific data-displays. You might even have students construct their own displays using scientific data you supply. In short, you'd probably try to have your students engage in activities that you believe would improve their ability to make accurate interpretations of scientific data-displays. Because of your less-than-clear understanding of the content standard in question, that's about all you *could* do. When a teacher has a rather general, unfocused grasp of a content standard, it almost always results in rather general, unfocused instructional plans.

However, let's say that you are a dutiful rule-follower, and you want to follow Rule 2 to the hilt. The rule calls for you to employ different sorts of classroom assessments to clarify the nature of any learning outcome. In our let's-pretend situation, this means you'd try to operationalize the state-sanctioned content standard by coming up with the kinds of assessments you could use to measure students' mastery of the standard.

Because the essence of the content standard is for students to interpret scientific data-displays, you'd need to figure out what kinds of test items might be appropriate to measure such a skill. Constructed response? Selected response? Well, ask yourself: What would students have to *do* to show that they could interpret these charts, tables, and graphs?

Let's say that after mulling the options for a while, you conclude there are three kinds of cognitive demands that, if used in concert, could help you determine your students' content mastery:

1. When presented with any scientific data-display, the student ought to be able to accurately summarize the major purpose(s) of that data-display.

2. If asked to use a given scientific data-display to arrive at particular kinds of conclusions (for example, to make specific comparisons of certain elements in the data-display) the student should be able to do so accurately.

3. When given a real or fictitious decision to be made, a decision for which a particular scientific data-display provides decision-

relevant information, the student will be able to make a reasonable, data-supported decision.

I expect you would realize you might effectively impose these three cognitive demands using both constructed-response and selected-response items. For instance, if you gave students oral or written test items for any of the three, the students could respond by using oral or written short answers. It would also be possible for you to whip up multiple-choice or even true-false items that would (perhaps less accurately) assess your students' abilities to carry out the three cognitive demands.

But the most important dividend of your efforts to clarify this science content standard is that you now have a better understanding of just what it is that your students need to be able to do in order to display mastery. With this enhanced understanding, you will almost certainly be able to design and deliver more appropriate instruction. For one thing, you'd probably make sure your students received ample guided and independent practice in dealing with all three of the cognitive demands you have isolated. Moreover, you'd be able to incorporate suitable cognitive modeling, showing the class how one would go about (1) isolating the chief purpose or purposes of each scientific table, figure, or graph encountered; (2) arriving at a requested set of data-based conclusions; and (3) using the data display's information to help resolve a presented decision-choice.

As this example shows, teachers who spend a bit of time thinking through how they might assess a somewhat loosely defined learning outcome—whether it's a too-general content standard, an ambiguous benchmark, or a gunky educational goal—can work backward from possible assessment items, clarify what the students must be able to do, and subsequently determine what students must be taught. Following Rule 2 provides several immediate instructional advantages:

• *Teachers' task analyses will be more accurate.* With a more precise fix on the learning outcome sought, it's easier for teachers to identify any enabling knowledge or subskills that students must acquire.

• *Teachers' in-class explanations will be clearer.* When teachers clearly understand what students are supposed to be able to do at the end of instruction, then the quality of the explanations provided to students is likely to be pretty good. These explanations will surely be more helpful and on-target than any delivered by a teacher who has only a foggy notion about what students are supposed to know and be able to do when instruction is complete.

• *Teachers' selected practice activities will be more germane.* In my teaching experience, the more relevant practice that students receive, the better they will usually perform. There's a ton of empirical research showing the positive link between "time on task" and student learning.

The Benefits of Assessment Diversity

We've talked about how analyzing the cognitive demands that a particular outcome's assessment tasks place on students can give a teacher a clearer picture of how to promote that outcome's mastery. Now we come to the other important aspect of Rule 2: its insistence on the use of diverse kinds of classroom assessment.

As educators, we want the students we teach to learn really worthwhile things, which is why I've been harping relentlessly on the need to focus most classroom instruction on truly significant learning outcomes. But teachers can trivialize even a significant outcome if they measure it in only one way.

Consider, for example, students' ability to solve age-appropriate mathematical problems by identifying a suitable solution strategy and carrying out all required computations correctly. This is a very significant mathematical outcome—something we want students to be able to do in the real world, in a variety of settings, and not just in response to an item on a test. What we are seeking, of course, is our students' *generalizable* mastery—their ability to apply the skills they've acquired in any situation they might encounter. I talked a little about generalizable mastery in Chapter 5.

Think of it this way: If we want to find out if students are capable of using a skill in a variety of settings, we must measure mastery of the skill in a variety of ways, and teach students to demonstrate mastery in those various ways. In contrast, if we use only one kind of test, and base instruction on that one-type test, we limit our ability to promote generalized skill mastery and our students' ability to attain it.

To illustrate, suppose a 4th grade teacher is trying to get students to master the skill of "comprehending a paragraph's main idea." This is an important skill, and certainly one that we would want students to be able to apply in a variety of circumstances. Now imagine that our hypothetical 4th grade teacher has only one way of assessing students' mastery of this skill: using classroom tests that present a paragraph from a story and a series of multiple-choice options, one of which reflects the paragraph's main idea.

Furthermore, the teacher has designed instruction with this single assessment method in mind. When introducing the skill, the teacher uses overhead slides featuring the paragraph-and-multiple-choice option format. Students' in-class practice and homework assignments also mirror this format.

When test-time rolls around, these students do very well indeed. Test results indicate they have mastered the skill. But what if one of these students was given a paragraph to read, then asked to generate "from scratch" a written or oral statement of the paragraph's main idea? My guess is that the student would stumble over this new and unfamiliar type of test. Has this skill *really* been mastered? Not in any generalizable way. The teacher's use of one-type testing has "limited" students' mastery; what's more, it's concealed from the teacher that a learning deficit even exists.

For this reason, Rule 2 stresses that the classroom assessments teachers use to must be *diverse*, meaning they must incorporate a variety of task-types—both constructed response and selected response. Think about what other item-types this 4th grade teacher might have used to impose the cognitive demand of "isolating the central message residing in a paragraph." If this teacher followed Rule 2 and used a more varied assessment to clarify this learning outcome, think about how the instructional approaches, explanations, and practice activities would change. For example, to the "read-the-paragraph and choose-the-best answer drill," the teacher might add independent reading, writing, and listening activities, along with further explanations focused on identifying author clues such as repetition and topic sentence placement. By giving students more diverse opportunities to develop and display their generalizable mastery of identifying main ideas in paragraphs, this teacher could more effectively promote and more accurately measure that learning.

Wrapping up our consideration of Rule 2, let me remind you that its main message is for teachers to use classroom assessments to help clarify their instructional targets. This clarification alone can yield potent payoffs in student learning. But, as the rule also stipulates, to get students to achieve a generalizable form of skill mastery, teachers must measure significant skills with more than one type of classroom test. Assessment diversity is dandy; one-type testing is troubling. Now let's roll on to the third rule.

~ Rule 3 ~

Make students' responses to classroom assessments central to your instructional decision making.

Testing takes place in virtually all teachers' classrooms. It's so prevalent that a visiting extraterrestrial might conclude that testing is one of the defining attributes of this planet's teachers. But *why* do teachers test? What do they do with the data classroom tests provide? We touched on this topic back in Chapter 2. Although there is growing awareness of testing's instructional implications, far too many teachers still test their students for grade dispensation and grade dispensation only. It's pretty deeply ingrained. Test-based grade giving has probably been taking place ever since Socrates asked Plato to write an essay about how he spent his summer vacation.

But using classroom tests *solely* to dish out students' grades is like using a laptop computer to keep your lap warm: There's such unfilled potential! And it's that unfilled potential in the classroom that I address in Rule 3. While I'm not suggesting that teachers ought to abandon test-based dispensation of grades altogether, Rule 3 makes it clear that classroom assessment has a higher calling—to improve the caliber of classroom instruction.

Students' test scores are *evidence*, and in my opinion, the single most important kind of evidence contributing to any instructional decision. Rule 3 encourages teachers to embrace this point of view. It tells them to regard classroom tests *primarily* as contributors of evidence for decisions about students' education, and only *secondarily* as determiners of students' grades. For many teachers, following this rule will require a meaningful rethinking of how they think about test scores and how they typically make instructional decisions about their students and themselves.

Student-Focused Instructional Decisions

Many of the instructional decisions a teacher must make deal directly with what's best for a specific student. "Should Jill be given additional help, possibly via peer tutoring, because she's having trouble in solving simultaneous-equation problems?" "Is Clyde ready to read more advanced essays analyzing the causes underlying the Civil War?" All too often, we find teachers reaching their instructional decisions somewhat intuitively, basing their conclusions on the quality of classroom discussion or the nature of a small number of questions and answers offered by a small number of students. No, I I'm not suggesting that most teachers currently make their instructional decisions on the basis of whim or Ouija board. What I *am* suggesting is that if possible, such decisions should be data-based, and should spring from a teacher's consideration of an individual student's test performance.

For example, it's clear how using a pretest to identify students' entry-level achievements can help a teacher decide whether any planned instruction aimed at a particular content standard should be skipped altogether because the students' pretest performances indicate they already have a solid mastery of that standard. On the other hand, pretest results might also tell a teacher that a specific student's entry-level skills are lots weaker than the teacher had thought. In this case, the evidence indicates that some serious remedial instruction is required.

Surely, you say, not *every* decision about a given student can be based on assessment evidence. Obviously, there will be all sorts of situations in which a teacher must rely on observations of the student, sometimes quite casual observations, rather than any sort of formal classroom assessment. But for the most part, I believe that instructional decisions about whether to, say, move a student on to other topics or spend more time on the topic at hand can be best made after consulting the student's performance on a relevant classroom test.

Teacher-Focused Instructional Decisions

Having been a teacher for many years, I know the tendency of teachers to make intuitive, data-free decisions about the quality of their instruction. I've done it myself, far too often. But judgments about the quality of a teacher's instruction should be based almost exclusively on *what happens to students as a consequence of that instruction.* Classroom assessment evidence can help teachers determine whether the instruction they provided was super, solid, or sickly.

Unless a teacher is teaching content that is totally new—content that no student in the class will have *ever* encountered before (and I can't think of many subjects where this would be the case outside of a first-year course in Latin)—the most direct way to arrive at an inference about instructional success is to employ some sort of pretest/post-test model, and compare what students knew and could do before they were taught with what they know and can do after instruction is complete. The *X*-factor, of course, is the teacher's educational impact.

Think back to the let's-pretend example presented with Rule 2, where you were a teacher trying to help your students become skilled interpreters of scientific data-displays. Let's say that at the end of a lengthy teaching unit focused on that skill, the unit exam reveals that most students haven't done particularly well. Closer inspection of the test results indicates that few of the students have mastered the third of the three types of cognitive demands present in the exam. This test evidence suggests that the instruction these children received was ineffective. As the teacher, you would need to reexamine the instructional activities you used, rethink the enabling subskills and knowledge required for this cognitive demand, then re-teach up a storm. Based on test results, your students "didn't get it." They need to be taught again—and this time, taught better.

Unfortunately, the classic pretest/post-test data-gathering design has some serious flaws as a measure of teaching success. I'll be dealing with those in the next chapter, when I introduce a more defensible data-gathering model and describe how teachers should use students' performances on classroom tests to arrive at accurate judgments about instructional effectiveness. But before we get to that, let's wrap up with my fourth and final rule for how to use classroom tests to enhance the caliber of instruction and meaningfully improve the quality of students' schooling.

~ Rule 4 ~

Regularly assess educationally significant student affect—but only to make inferences about groups of students, not individual students.

If teachers teach children to master a certain subject matter but do so in a manner that leads those youngsters to hate the material they've mastered, it might have been better to have never tackled the subject in the first place. Children who have been drilled relentlessly so they can do multiplication tables like a magician may, unfortunately, end up despising anything numerical—and being defiantly and permanently anti-math by the age of 9. That's an educational tragedy. If I were obliged to choose between students' love of learning and their mastery of any collection of cognitive content standards, I'd choose the former every time.

I have just revealed my sentiments about the importance of *affect*. When we educators speak of affect, we are generally referring to students' attitudes, interests, and values. I'm especially concerned with attitudes and interests, although I confess I wouldn't mind if our schools were able to nurture students' increased valuing of justice, honesty, and integrity. (But that's a different book.) In Rule 4, I've restricted myself to advocating that teachers assess what I call *educationally significant* affect—variables such as such as students' attitudes toward learning, their interest in particular sub-jects, and their confidence in being able to use significant school-taught skills such as those associated with written and oral commu-nication. Educationally significant affective evidence can illuminate teachers' instructional decisions, and can even cast light on the effectiveness of teachers' instructional activities.

Rule 4 also stresses that affect should be "routinely" assessed—that is, measured on a regular and continuing basis, so that teachers might monitor how student affect changes over time, in response to what's going on in the classroom. I believe in affective pre-assessment and post-assessment, as well as periodic, en route affec-tive measurement. One-time-only affective assessment is better than nothing, but there's just not much information about instructional ef-fectiveness to be had from a single affective assessment.

Affective Inferences

Note that Rule 4 states very explicitly students' responses to affective assessments should be used to arrive at group-focused rather than individual-focused inferences. In other words, it would be appropri-ate for a teacher to infer that "based on my students' responses to af-fective inventories, *their* interest in studying science is increasing." Conversely, it would *not* be appropriate for that teacher to infer that "based on Johnny's response to a self-report affective inventory, *his* interest in studying science is increasing."

The reason to avoid individual-focused inferences stems from the nature of affective assessment instruments. As a practical matter, teachers who want to measure students' affect must usually rely on *self-report inventories.* These inventories typically present students with statements and ask the students to indicate the degree to which they agree or disagree with each statement. Here are a few examples of the kinds of statements you'd find on self-report affective inventories:

- "I often would rather read a book than watch TV."
- "Social studies is an interesting subject for me."
- "I don't feel comfortable if I have to make an oral report."
- "I think most scientists probably have very boring careers."

Obviously, it is important that students respond honestly when they mark "strongly agree" for one statement and "disagree" for another. It's all about validity. Dishonest responses could lead the teacher to make invalid inferences, which would lead to poor instructional decisions. The best way to promote student honesty is to assure them that their responses will be totally anonymous. But if there's any way of identifying a student's response, then you can be sure that many students will supply a load of "socially desirable" responses—that is, responses reflecting what they think the teacher will want to see.

This quest for honesty—and for valid affective inferences—means teachers must employ *anonymous* self-report affective inventories. Genuine anonymity means there can be *no names* and *no written comments* on any self-report inventory, only marks. Moreover, students must be sure that the method of collecting the completed inventories provides no way of tracing their responses. Teachers should remain seated while students are filling out affective inventories (rather than strolling around the room), and should provide sealed, secret ballot-type collection boxes with a small opening where students can insert their completed inventories.

My experience suggests that even when the procedure for completing affective inventories is completely cloaked in anonymity, some students will still make their responses either more positive than they should be ("good-goody" students will always do this) or more negative than they should be (cunning students know how to take revenge on a teacher). However, when the teacher adds up all the responses for an entire class, the too-positive and too-negative responses tend to cancel each other out, at least to some degree. This "natural balancing" provides all the more reason why educators' affective inferences about students must be made about *groups* of students (a whole class or the entire student body) and not *individual* students.

Affect-Powered Instructional Decisions

All affective data gathering should be carried out for the purpose of improving the caliber of instructional decisions. When teachers choose the items to include in any affective assessment device, each item's responses should reflect a readily discernible implication for a subsequent instructional decision.

For example, if an affective pre-assessment shows that a class of 4th graders is fairly uninterested in social studies, but a midyear assessment indicates that interest in social studies has become stronger, then the teacher has reason to believe that the social studies content being provided is pretty good, at least on the criterion of interest-generation. Whatever is going on with respect to affect regarding social studies seems to be working. On the other hand, if periodic measures of students' joy in reading (based, for example, on self-report inventories given every two months) show that students' pleasure in their reading continues to decline, then the teacher should decide to alter the reading instruction, which appears to be sapping students' pleasure in reading. The teacher might try installing some reading-related activities that are patently intended to allow students to have reading-based fun. One option might be small-group games in which students use the conclusions drawn from their reading. The idea is to develop instructional activities that make reading *itself* more enjoyable, rather than sugarcoating reading activities so they're more palatable.

One affective measure that I have always found very illuminating in my own instructional decisions is students' expressed confidence in being able to perform certain cognitive skills. There is a positive relationship (although not perfect, to be sure) between students' ability to carry out skills and their expressed confidence in being able to do so. I often use confidence inventories that ask students to choose between options varying from "very confident" to "not at all confident" for skills such as their ability to solve word problems in math class or their ability to fill out job application forms.

When collected on a group basis, students' affect regarding their own capabilities can offer teachers useful insight regarding the degree to which the students actually possess the skills listed on the inventory. In a sense, the evidence from students' anonymously expressed confidence in performing certain skills serves as a proxy for the evidence that might be garnered by using actual (and usually more time-consuming) assessments of those same skills.

The main message of Rule 4 is that teachers can gain instructional guidance from valid affective-focused inferences just as readily as they can from valid cognitive-focused inferences. The trick for teachers, of course, is to learn how to create suitable affective data-gathering instruments.

I have no illusions about the potency of this chapter's brief treatment of affective measurement. Clearly, those who would employ affective measurement in the classroom need to learn more about how to do it well. One of the books I've listed in the References and Resources section (Anderson & Bourke, 2000) deals exclusively with affective assessment. It is a winner. Another, written by me (Popham, in press), has a good chapter about affective assessment and some stealable examples of age-appropriate, self-report affective inventories.

These Rules Will Work

My objective for this chapter was to set down some simple rules that can help teachers deliver the sort of instruction that helps children learn better. For many teachers, considering classroom assessment in this instructionally-oriented way is a new and different thing. These are the teachers I most hope to reach.

My message to these folks is this: If your major classroom assessments, even of the affective variety, focus on a modest number of significant outcomes; if you use the assessments themselves to clarify your understanding of the outcomes sought; and if you rely heavily on students' responses to guide your instructional decisions . . . then *your students will learn better.* That's a pretty good outcome.

Collecting Credible Evidence of Instructional Effectiveness

7

For all the reasons we discussed in earlier chapters, students' scores on existing standardized achievement tests do not provide an accurate way of judging how well teachers are teaching. There are mismatches between what's tested and what's taught. The quest for score-spread leads to the elimination of many items measuring important, teacher-stressed content. And confounded causality occurs because the items on such tests measure not only what's learned in school, but also what's learned outside of school, as well as students' inherited academic aptitudes.

But if reliance on standardized achievement tests isn't the answer to determining teachers' instructional success, what is? Educators all over the land are facing this question, and we aren't finding any easy answers. Our commitment to our students inspires us to want to provide the strongest and most effective instruction possible. As professionals, we agree that we should be accountable for the quality of instruction we deliver. We're also interested in getting due credit for our successes. How do we get an accurate picture of our own effectiveness? And how can we demonstrate to parents, policymakers, and the public-at-large that we're doing our jobs? After all, there's no going back to the days where heartfelt reassurances from school officials could convince citizens that all was right in U.S. classrooms. We're living in an era that requires evidence.

I'm here to help. In this chapter, I'm going talk about how educators can use assessment to assemble evidence of instructional effectiveness. I'll first tackle the issue from the perspective of a classroom teacher, then adjust the focus and examine ways to gauge the success of an entire school staff or a district staff. Throughout, my suggestions will be guided by one crucial, eight-letter word, the second in this chapter's title. That word is *credible*. Educators need to face the troubling reality that neither the public nor our elected officials trust us when we say, "We're doing a great job!" Because our audience is a skeptical one, the evidence we collect regarding our effectiveness must be significant and it must be thoroughly substantiated. It must be credible enough to convince the incredulous. Let's begin by looking at how teachers might collect evidence to inform themselves—and other interested parties—about the quality of instruction they deliver.

Evidence of a Teacher's Instructional Effectiveness

Effective educators change children. We help them acquire skills and knowledge that they didn't have before our instruction. We turn a group of youngsters who are disdainful of science into a collection of would-be scientists. We create better readers. We develop stronger thinkers. Any important or believable evidence about a teacher's instructional prowess needs to center on the issue of whether students have been changed.

The nature of the changes, of course, must be carefully considered. If teachers produce compelling evidence that they've brought about trifling changes, few sensible people will get very excited. Suppose a 4th grade teacher collected pretest–to–post-test evidence that students who started the school year incapable of spelling the word "similar" can now, after nine months of intense teaching, spell the word correctly. Would anyone be ecstatic over such a trivial triumph? Of course not.

Thus, the first task for teachers who hope to use classroom assessments to generate evidence of their instructional effectiveness is to select the learning outcomes they plan to collect evidence about. Here are some guidelines on the kinds of student changes teachers should consider documenting through assessment.

Cognitive Gains

Because most people consider cognitive growth to be the most significant change that education can impart, I believe that *most* of the evidence teachers collect should deal with student gains in cognitive skills—the more demanding, the better.

Think back to the sets of rules I rolled out in Chapters 5 and 6, which stressed that test developers and classroom teachers should identify and measure a small number of major cognitive outcomes. That's precisely what I'm advocating here. As a teacher hoping to use classroom tests to gauge the effectiveness of your own instruction, wouldn't you be most interested in finding out how well your instruction helps students achieve the outcomes you consider to be the most important? What would you rather be sure of teaching well: a student's skill in solving high-level mathematical problems or a student's skill in adding pairs of double-digit numbers?

Similarly, with calls for accountability coming down from all sides, teachers have an extrinsic motivation for collecting compelling and credible evaluative data to illustrate their instructional effectiveness. This is not the time to prove we know how to teach ho-hum skills. I'd like to see teachers collect solid evidence that their students have mastered really powerful cognitive skills—skills so powerful that evidence of students' increased achievement will wow principals, parents, and policymakers.

Knowledge Outcomes

I've been pretty clear on what I consider to be the lesser importance of knowledge-only outcomes. However, teachers can measure and include students' gains in knowledge as evidence of instructional effectiveness, provided that the body of knowledge taught is both important and extensive. Suppose a 4th grade teacher collected evidence showing that before instruction, students could spell correctly only 30 percent of a set of 500 tough-to-spell words, but after instruction, they could spell 95 percent of those words. That's an impressive achievement—one that might convince parents and administrators that those students had received some first-class instruction.

Affective Outcomes

Teachers too often overlook affective outcomes as a source for evidence of instructional effectiveness. If a teacher's class indicates little interest in leisure reading before instruction, but registers scads of enthusiasm for leisure reading after instruction, that's darn good evaluative data. That teacher is doing something right. Perhaps students indicated great uneasiness about giving oral reports at the start of a school year, but after lots of guided practice in oral report presentation, they now indicate that they feel very confident about giving such reports. This evidence also falls into the "darn good" category, and it makes a strong case for the teacher's instructional ability.

A Reminder About Basic Assessment Literacy

Once a teacher has decided on the knowledge, skills, or affective outcomes to be measured, the second task is to figure out how to measure those outcomes. And it's at this point that the last chapter's "pre-rule rule" makes a return appearance. Here it is again:

> **Teachers, and those who work with them, should familiarize themselves with the fundamentals of classroom assessment.**

Classroom assessments are a vital component of any serious evidence gathering. If a teacher does not know how to construct routine classroom assessments, that teacher should *not* be excused from duty and assigned to a decade of supervising bake sales. That teacher should be directed to read a textbook on classroom assessment and acquire the necessary skills.

The rest of this chapter assumes that teachers either know how to construct the kinds of classroom assessments routinely required or can select such assessments sensibly from a set of available options—say, a state-developed set of classroom tests linked to the state's approved content standards. Classroom tests can be built or borrowed, but they are an indispensable tool for demonstrating instructional effectiveness.

Pretest/Post-Test Perils

At the most rudimentary level, it would seem that if you wanted to see whether students have changed as a consequence of a teacher's instruction, you'd simply test the students on the identified content before instruction, then test them again when instruction is over. A simple comparison between the pretests and the post-tests would "tell the tale." Nice try, but no cigar.

Take a look at the traditional pretest/post-test model in Figure 7.1. This elementary data-gathering design is what most people turn to when they want to see "if instruction makes any difference." Unfortunately, the traditional pretest/post-test design doesn't work—at least, it doesn't work if you're trying to determine whether teachers have been effective.

The Reactive Effect

The major problem with the traditional pretest/post-test design is that when students take a pretest, they often become sensitized to its content. As a consequence, when students receive instruction (after the pretesting is over), they tend to focus on the things they recall from the pretest. This response, technically known as the *reactive effect* of pretesting, makes it less clear if the teacher's instruction is really working.

To keep the illustration simple, assume that a 10-item pretest has been used, and that each item asks students to write a brief, one-paragraph answer. Students are a clever crowd. If they recall a pretest item on which they struck out, they may be atypically alert when, several weeks later, the teacher treats the topic that item addressed. On the post-test, the teacher notes a big jump in the number of students who responded satisfactorily to this item. Was it the teacher's stellar instruction that caused this effect, or does the teacher's instruction merely *appear* effective because the pretest item spurred student interest?

Even worse, suppose that after flopping on several of the pretest's 10 items, several students went home and read up on the topics addressed (because, as any savvy student can tell you, where there's a pretest, there's certain to be post-test waiting in the wings). They could pick up the information necessary to provide correct answers on the post-test before the teacher begins test-relevant instruction. If the pretest were readministered, they might score 100 percent correct *without having been taught.* Cunning devils!

7.1　**A Traditional Pretest/Post-Test Data Gathering Design**

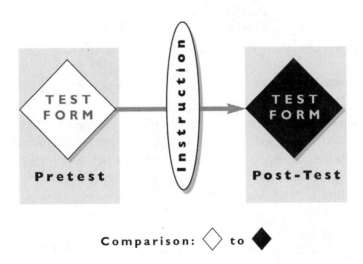

Can This Design Be Saved?

To circumvent pretesting's reactive effect (and prevent clever students from obscuring the true impact of instruction) some teachers try to create a post-test that is different from the pretest, but equal in terms of difficulty. Unfortunately, these attempts are almost never successful: The pretest and post-test will almost surely differ in difficulty. For about a decade, I headed a test-development group that was occasionally obliged to come up with two "equidifficult" test forms. We had lots of people working on this task, lots of time to do it, and lots of dollars to support our efforts. Yet we succeeded only some of the time. This seemingly simple task is much tougher than you would think; all sorts of tryouts and revision go into creating two genuinely equidifficult test forms.

Of course, when teachers use pretests and post-tests of *differing* difficulties, all sorts of crazy things can occur. What happens, for instance, if the post-test is easier than the pretest? Students' scores may go up, but these increases will probably reflect the relative softness of the post-test rather than genuine learning. And how about a tougher post-test than pretest? Students' scores may actually dip—and that dip is likely to take place even if the teacher has been dishing out superlative instruction.

No, using a different pretest and post-test doesn't solve the problem of reactive impact and savvy students, and despite its intuitive appeal, the traditional pretest/post-test data-gathering design is unable to supply credible evidence regarding a teacher's instructional effectiveness.

A Different Approach to Data Gathering

Because of the difficulties associated with the traditional pretest/post-test design, I recommend that teachers use a quite different sort of data-gathering approach. Called the *split-and-switch design*, it's a variation on the classic pretest/post-test method, specifically calculated for teachers who want to determine their own effectiveness. The design is illustrated in Figure 7.2. Let me explain how it works and why it will provide teachers the level of clarity and credibility they seek.

7.2   A Split-and-Switch Version of the Pretest/Post-Test Design

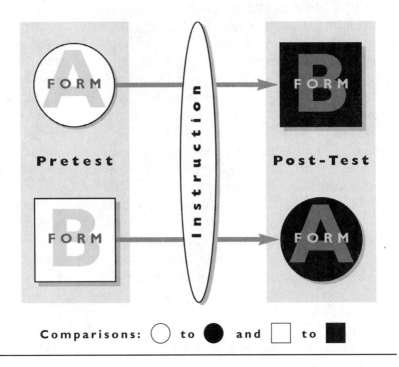

In the split-and-switch design, the teacher creates two forms of a test, somewhat similar in difficulty. The teacher then splits the class into two halves. One half of the class takes uses the first form as a pretest and the other half of the class uses the second form as a pretest. The teacher teaches up a storm, then switches the half-classes so that each group uses the *other* form as their post-test. As the figure illustrates, Half-Class 1 takes Form A as a pretest and Form B as a post-test; Half-Class 2 takes Form B as a pretest and Form A as a post-test. After blind-scoring all Form As (pretests and post-tests mixed together) and all Form Bs (similarly scrambled), the teacher compares the pretest and post-test scores on Form A and the pretest and post-test scores on Form B.

The split-and-switch design assumes that a sample of roughly half the teacher's students will provide a reasonable approximation of how well the whole class would have scored on a test. In essence, the split-and-switch design, with its Form A pretest/post-test contrast and Form B pretest/post-test contrast, gives the teacher two sets of data to document how much students have learned. More importantly, the split-and-switch has none of the reactivity problems associated with the traditional pretest/post-test data-gathering design. Pretest reactivity is not an issue because no student uses the same test form twice. Although students' memory of pretest items may pique their interest in the subject matter or lead them to look up an answer at home, it won't translate directly into a higher score on the post-test. In addition, there's no concern about pretest/post-test variations in difficulty. Form A as a pretest is exactly equidifficult to Form A as a post-test, because, well, it's the same test (only the test-takers have changed).

Step-by-Step Through the Split-and-Switch

Below, I've set out 12 steps for teachers interested in trying this data-gathering approach. As you probably know, 12-step programs have helped a lot of people overcome addictions. Think of the 12 steps of the split-and-switch as a "program" that can help educators overcome the absence of credible evaluative data.

1. *Start with two forms of an assessment.* You can use a traditional selected-response test (multiple choice) or a more elaborate constructed-response performance test (say, a writing sample), complete with a rubric. The assessment can also consist of anonymously submitted affective inventories. The two forms do not need to be exactly equidifficult, although they both must measure a student's mastery of the *same* skill, body of knowledge, or affective variable (and ideally, the outcomes measured should be important ones). Label one form "Form A" and the other "Form B." I should mention it's wise to downplay the use of two different test forms. Both forms, for example, should use the same color of paper. You want to avoid creating curiosity about what is on "the other test."

2. *Lay the foundation for blind-scoring.* Pretest and post-test responses will be scored together. Your objective is to make sure that when student responses are scored, the person scoring them (you or someone else) will not be able to tell which are pretests and which are post-tests. Make enough copies of both Form A and Form B to serve as pretests and post-tests. Remember to print pretests and post-tests on the same color paper.

3. *Make the split.* To establish your two sample groups, I suggest that you simply count the number of students in your class (for example, 30), and then split them into two equal groups according to your alphabetical class roster. For example, the first 15 students should receive Form A as a pretest and the next 15 should receive Form B as a pretest.

4. *Establish the motivation.* Try to get your students to do well on both the pretest (and later on, the post-test) by stressing the significance of the test they're about to take. For the pretest, you may want to provide some small grade or incentive for your students. Ideally, students' motivation levels should be similar for both the pretest and the post-test.

5. *Administer the pretest.* As you distribute the pretest forms to your students, tell them to write their names on their responses (preferably on the back of the test's last page) *but not a date.*

6. *Collect and code the pretests.* Separate the collected pretests into Form A and Form B. Next, using a code that only you know, mark each pretest response unobtrusively (for instance, on the back of the last page) so that *after* the papers have been scored they can be identified as pretests. This is imperative, or the whole split-and-switch design blows sky high. Any coding approach will work as long as you can subsequently tell how to separate pretest and post-test responses once they have been scored. (I know some teachers who put a series of seemingly random numbers on the back of each test. To indicate a pretest, they'll use an even number as the second in the series; to indicate a post-test, the second number will be odd.) Once the papers have been coded, put the pretest responses in your files. If, before filing the responses, you want to use the pretests to get a fix on your students' status at the outset of instruction, go to it.

Just be sure not to *write* anything on the pretests.

7. *Teach.* Next, teach as effectively as you can toward the skill, body of knowledge, or affect being assessed via the two test forms, but do not teach toward the *particular* tasks or items being used for pretests and post-tests. Your objective is to promote improvements in students' skill, knowledge, or affect, not students' familiarity with a given test's particulars. If you teach toward the actual test forms, what you'll get is an altogether inaccurate picture of students' growth.

8. *Make the switch and administer the post-test.* At post-test time, 'reverse the pretest form distribution. Students who took Form A as a pretest, get Form B as a post-test; students who took Form B as a pretest, take Form A as a post-test. Again, make sure students do not put a date on their test responses.

9. *Collect and code the post-tests.* After all post-tests have been collected, separate them into Forms A and B. Then, using a scheme similar to the one you used on the pretests, code the post-tests so they can be distinguished from the pretests. If students have transferred into your class so recently that you do not believe they have had time to be properly taught, I'd exclude those students' responses from the scoring.

10. *Combine and score.* Combine the Form A pretests with the Form A post-tests, and the Form B pretests with the Form B post-tests. Shuffle, if desired. You may want to score the mixed-together responses yourself (Form A, then Form B), or you may want to call on colleagues or even parents to supply truly nonpartisan scoring. Teachers should score their students' responses only if they truly can't tell, from appearance alone, which responses are pretests and which are post-tests. (Many teachers will have used the pretests to guide them instructionally, so they may recognize particular responses as pretests. I usually recommend having an outside party score the mixed-together papers. More on this shortly.)

11. *Separate, calculate, and contrast.* Once all student responses have been scored, it's time to determine the overall averages for the pretests and the post-tests. Beginning with the Form As, use your coding system to separate the pretests and post-tests. If you're using a selected-response test, compute the average numerical scores for

the pretests, then the post-tests. If you're using a constructed-response test, calculate the percentage of pretests, then post-tests assigned to each of your quality-level categories ("Distinguished," "Proficient," and so on). For affective self-report inventories, employ whatever scoring scheme is required. Repeat the separation and calculation process for Form B. Then contrast students' pretest performances with their post-test performances. Remember, you will have two pretest–to–post-test contrasts (Forms A and B), not just one.

12. *Apply as desired.* It is possible to use the post-tests (the non-affective ones) for grading. If you plan to do so, make sure that the two test forms are approximately equal in difficulty. If not, take any difficulty differences into consideration when assigning grades. Of course, the application we're most interested in is what these scores reveal about instructional effectiveness. Consider your students' pretest/post-test changes. If the post-test scores show little gain, you should reconsider your instructional activities related to what the assessments measure. If you find that the post-tests reflect whopping big gains, you might want to share the results with a principal, department head, or any living soul within shouting distance! Be even prouder of yourself if the tests were blind-scored by nonpartisans.

A Time-Saving Tip for Affective Assessment

If you plan to use the split-and-switch design with affective assessment instruments—for example, a 20-item self-report attitude inventory—you can either create two different 20-item forms (usually a real pain) or you can simply split the 20-item inventory into two half-tests of 10 items each. This procedure, technically referred to as *item sampling*, works delightfully. Remember, when employing affective assessment, a teacher is concerned with group-focused inferences—not inferences about individual students. When the half-tests have been scored, you can simply add these scores together to generate a whole-test affective estimate for the entire class.

Tips for Split-and-Switch Scoring

For an extra measure of reliability (and credibility), I do recommend teachers find an outside party to handle the blind-scoring of split-

and-switch evidence. Other teachers are a popular choice for impartial scorers. (For even more credibility, you might consider using teachers from another school.) Parent volunteers also make ideal nonpartisan scorers. For "objectively scoreable" tests, such as those involving selected-response items, there's little difficulty in finding parents ready to chip in. For judging students' higher-level skills—for example, the kind of skill you might measure with a performance test—all you need do is explain to parent scorers how a rubric works and how to use the rubric to score those responses.

Another of the split-and-switch data-gathering design's attractive features is that you don't need to have scorers who bring identical scoring standards to the enterprise. To illustrate, suppose Mother Muggins and Father Fisher are two parent volunteer scorers. Mother M. is a "tough" scorer, while Father F. is soft as a satin bedspread. Because the pretests and post-tests are mixed together, Mother M.'s scoring stringency will come crashing down on students in an even-handed manner. The same is true for Father F.'s lenient standards; he'll score the pretests as kindly as he'll score the post-tests. Consequently, when the pretests and post-tests have been sorted out, the same scoring standards will have been applied to both, and the difference in average scores will not be affected by the scorers' biases.

What the Scores Mean

If, on the basis of blind-scoring, students' post-tests are judged to be meaningfully better than their pretests, teachers should take real pride in this accomplishment—especially if a significant learning outcome is being measured. The reason for such pride is that there's a wrinkle in the split-and-switch design that tends to minimize the measured degree of pretest–to–post-test improvement. Remember, students are randomly assigned to the two half-classes. And the result of such random assignment is that some of a teacher's most able students will be completing pretest Form A and some will be completing pretest Form B. Even without the benefit of formal instruction, these superstar students can often wend their way through a pretest and make it look as though it were a post-test. The superstars' scores, when factored into the average, will tend to raise both groups' pretest scores. Of course, those same superstars will also be taking both forms of the post-test, but by that time, the rest of the students will have received instruction and the contrast in scores won't be as dramatic. Substantial pretest–to–post-test growth on one or both of the two test forms indicates that this "superstar pretest bias" has been overridden by instruction. As I suggested, teachers who get striking pretest–to–post-test gains should be rightfully proud.

And if there are no meaningful gains, what does this signify? For example, what does it mean if you detect no difference between students' pretest and post-test performances on either of the two test forms? Of course, there's always the possibility that the small sample of students involved was not stable enough to yield an accurate picture of what went on in class. But my usual interpretation of a no-difference result is that the instruction wasn't all that wonderful.

I've seen the split-and-switch design used to gather data that indicated substantial pretest–to–post-test gains (see Popham, 2000b). I've also seen it generate results indicative of ineffective instruction. In the latter situation, I was able to speak to some of the teachers who hadn't come up with positive results. In candid, off-the-record conversations, these teachers admitted to me that they hadn't taught very skillfully; that is, they felt they had not addressed with sufficient seriousness the particular cognitive skill to be taught. As a group, these teachers wanted another crack at the split-and-switch model so they could show more success.

The Possibility of Subversion (and What to Do About It)

A word of caution. Like most other data-gathering approaches, the spilt-and-switch design can be subverted by teachers with subversion in mind. One of the most direct ways a teacher can illegitimately boost students' pretest–to–post-test gains is by teaching directly toward the actual *items* on both test forms. Item-focused teaching violates the essence of this evidence-producing design, inflates the post-test scores, and makes it impossible to draw valid inferences about students' status with respect to whatever the test forms are attempting to represent.

There are only two ways of dealing with subversion of the

split-and-switch design. School and district-level instructional leaders can stress and re-stress that any sort of item-focused teaching short-changes the children. They can also inform teachers that as a safeguard against any item-specific teaching, randomly selected students may be interviewed after the post-test to determine whether any sort of item-specific teaching transpired. My intuition is that such a student-check strategy will rarely, if ever, be needed, but its possibility may act as a deterrent to potential "subverters." I think most teachers will play the split-and-switch game by the rules, particularly if the test is specifically designed to help them instructionally, as discussed in Chapter 6.

Proof for the Educator

The split-and-switch design provides teachers with a great way to find out for themselves how much their students have learned. As mentioned in the last chapter, it's temptingly easy for teachers to conclude that their instruction "worked." This design, with its blind-scoring of mixed-together pretests and post-tests, supplies a more definitive answer to the question, "Was my instruction truly effective?"

Given the rather small sample sizes involved, this design is by no means a definitive, always accurate, never-miss way of assembling evidence regarding a teacher's success. But, as you know, life typically presents us with choices. The choice in this instance is whether to collect relevant data using a strong, albeit less than perfect, data-gathering approach, or not to collect relevant data at all. One exception, though: If a teacher's class is too small for the split-and-switch to be an accurate predictor of whole class achievement (fewer than 20 students), I'd recommend using a traditional pretest/post-test model, although I would insist that students' responses be blind-scored (preferably by objective outsiders).

Still, factoring in all the positive features of the split-and-switch design, I think it can be the data-gathering model of choice for most classroom teachers who want to get a reasonably rigorous fix on whether their instruction worked. I've spoken with a number of teachers who use the split-and-switch data-gathering design regularly. Although they confess to having found it a bit threatening the first time they used it, they now swear by it. This novel data-gathering device really can be an objective, tough-minded way for teachers to document how well they're teaching.

Proof for the World

As I've indicated numerous times in this book, today's accountability pressures oblige teachers to come up with evidence of effectiveness that the rest of the world will pay attention to. The split-and-switch design can help you out here, too, particularly if you follow my guidelines for measuring important learning outcomes and make sure students' mixed-together pretests and post-tests are blind-scored by nonpartisans. If you're a teacher who wants evidence of educational effectiveness to be taken seriously, why not give this technique a try?

Evidence of School or District Instructional Success

Let's turn now to an even more vexing question: How do educators assemble evidence to evaluate instructional quality in an entire school, or even an entire district? There are parallels between the approaches that work in a classroom and the approaches we need for a larger-scale educational setting. The most striking similarity to consider when gathering any evidence of instructional quality is that it's going to be of interest to the same essential, two-part audience: the educators and the rest of the world.

Educators at all levels are interested in attaining decent evidence of their effectiveness so that they may (1) do a better job of teaching the students, and (2) show the rest of the world that they are, in fact, doing a good job. In short, whether at a classroom, school, district, or even a national level, the two major motivations for evaluating instructional quality are *instructional improvement* and *accountability*. Moreover, for purposes of accountability, evidence of instructional effectiveness at any level must be credible.

But there are also important practical differences between the appraisal of instructional quality at the classroom level and its appraisal at school or district levels. Teachers typically collect evaluative evidence of instructional quality for themselves and because they want do it (although, as teacher-targeted accountability pressures continue to increase, this may soon be changing). In contrast—at least for now—school-site administrators and district administrators are obliged to carry out evaluations of educational effectiveness for somebody else. School principals collect evaluative evidence for superintendents. Superintendents collect evaluative evidence for school boards. The higher the level, the more powerful the audience reviewing the evidence is likely to be—and the more likely it is that this audience will include "the rest of the world." For this reason, it's even more essential that the evidence provided be credible.

Fortunately, the higher the level, the more resources are likely to be devoted to support any evaluative operation. For individual teachers with lesson plans to get through and homework to grade, elaborate data gathering can be a burden. This kind of data gathering is much easier to carry out at the school level, and easier still at the district level, where there are often designated specialists devoted to the task full time.

With that said, let's take a closer look at how school or district administrators called upon to present evidence of large-scale instructional equality to an external auditing authority might go about collecting the data they need. These administrators face some formidable evaluative obstacles.

Build a Powerful Case

When I was growing up, my television hero was Perry Mason, an affable lawyer of remarkable courtroom prowess. Viewers never had to wonder whether Perry's client was innocent; that was a given. What we watched for was to see how this superlitigator built his case. It was the quality of his defense that always delivered the jury's "not guilty" verdict (usually followed in milliseconds by the apprehension of the real culprit, conveniently present in the courtroom).

My recommendation to educators who are responsible for school-level or district-level evaluation of educational effectiveness is to follow Perry Mason's strategy: *Build a powerful case!* More specifically, build a powerful case based on as much pertinent and credible evidence as you can amass.

It's important to note that this activity also requires the integrity of a Perry Mason. The evidence administrators seek out must lead to a *truthful* appraisal of the effectiveness of the instruction under consideration. They aren't in the public relations game, wherein they must polish a potato, then pass it off as an apple. If students are being badly taught, educators need to know so that the teaching can be repaired. Accountability that will help children must be *honest* accountability. And to make that accountability honest, the administrator must assemble a solid array of accurate, convincing evidence, culled from a variety of sources.

The idea that any sort of important educational decision shouldn't be based on a single source of data is not exactly a new thought. In recent years, a galaxy of reputable individuals and organizations (including the American Educational Research Association and the American Psychological Association) have made us aware that basing an educational decision on a single datapoint—on test scores from a single test, for instance—is flat-out folly. Educators should *never* rely on a single criterion when arriving at any sort of important decision.

And that's exactly the mentality an educational administrator must adopt when mapping out a plan to collect evidence regarding educational quality. It's important to note that the *kinds of evidence* about educational quality available in one school or district setting can differ significantly from the kinds that are available in another. Administrators must (1) build an honest case using all the credible evidence they have at their disposal, and (2) present the case in a reader-friendly, plain-talk sort of report. An administrator's goal should always be to build an accurate, understandable appraisal of instructional quality that will make sense to those who should have such information. The following subsections discuss sources of evidence for those who want to put together a strong local evaluative case.

Scores from the *Right Kind* of Large-Scale Test

Large-scale achievement tests can yield useful data about the status of students' learning and the quality of schooling they receive, *provided that these tests have been created in accordance with strict, instructionally facilitative rules*, such as those in Chapter 5. To be a suitable source of evidence, large-scale achievement tests must simultaneously (1) measure the most important learning outcomes to be taught and (2) provide clarity for teachers about what those outcomes are. Having reached this stage of the book, you know the kinds of standardized tests so widely used throughout the United States do not meet these criteria.

What if you're an administrator looking for evidence of your school's or district's instructional success and the only large-scale achievement tests available are the traditionally built, off-the-shelf, nationally standardized ones—or their state-customized counterparts that function much the same way? Better to use no large-scale assessment data at all than to rely on the misleading evidence yielded by these unsound tests.

It will take some serious effort to enhance the assessment literacy of educational policymakers before we will see the introduction of the right kinds of achievement tests, either locally or nationally. In the final chapter, I'll suggest how educators might stimulate the creation of suitable large-scale achievement tests that can give us an accurate picture of student learning and instructional effectiveness. Stay tuned.

Large-Scale Aggregate Split-and-Switch Evidence

An aggregation of an entire school or entire district's per-teacher split-and-switch evidence can make a particularly compelling case for instructional effectiveness, especially if students' responses have been blind-scored by nonpartisan judges, such as parents or other members of the community. I recommend administrators relay brief summaries of pretest/post-test studies to policymakers and to parents, who should also receive copies of their own children's blind-scored pretests and post-tests.

I've observed two such districtwide applications of the

split-and-switch data-gathering design. One produced such strong evidence of educational effectiveness that I was asked to write up the results in a national journal (Popham, 2000b). The results of the other showed as many students making pretest–to–post-test losses as making pretest–to–post-test gains. (Interestingly, the educators in that second district did *not* ask me to write up their results.)

Large-Scale Affective Evidence

School- and district-level assessment of affect can also provide convincing evidence of instructional success. For example, if students' expressed confidence in being able to carry out significant cognitive skills increases from pretest–to–post-test, I believe there's a strong likelihood that students' actual possession of those skills has been enhanced during that period. And if administrators produce evidence that students exhibit an increasingly positive attitude toward science, mathematics, or other intimidating subjects, that's powerful support for a claim of instructional success. Here are a few more examples of affective targets administrators might want to measure:

- Positive attitude toward learning.
- Positive attitude toward volitional reading.
- Interest in civic affairs.
- A belief in the safety of a given school's environment.

All my previous warnings regarding affective assessment still hold. Large-scale assessments of affect must always focus on group rather than individual inferences. Anonymity of data collection, both real and perceived, is a must. And of course, for evaluative purposes, be sure to assess only those affective variables that are both important and noncontroversial. If parents come forward wanting to eliminate a school- or district-level affective assessment because "it's messing with moral values," then that assessment is measuring the wrong affective variables. I find it hard to believe that anyone other than a trained naysayer would object to affective assessments that measure children's interest in reading or their confidence in being able to make oral presentations to their classmates.

The real advantage of this sort of large-scale affective assessment is that when only group-focused inferences are considered, we can engage in all sorts of sampling, both person-sampling and item-sampling, yet get an accurate fix on the affective dispositions of large groups of students.

Powerful Nontest Evidence

Who says that all evidence of school quality has to come from tests? If I were an administrator, I'd also be sure to use evidence based on quality-relevant nontest indicators, such as attendance rates and tardiness frequency. Keep in mind that the nature of the most appropriate nontest evidence usually changes from setting to setting. For instance, if we are evaluating instructional quality in an academically oriented high school, we might derive legitimate evaluative insights from (1) the number of students who enroll in (and, possibly, pass) advanced placement courses, or (2) the number of students who subsequently attend a four-year college. In schools that are less academically oriented, we might direct our evaluative attention to (1) the reduction of student-authored graffiti, or (2) frequency of participation in school-sponsored afterschool activities. The idea is that in a given school or district, educators must decide which nontest indicators can help illuminate the caliber of instruction being provided. And, of course, educators must select the kinds of nontest indicators that will withstand the scrutiny of skeptics. Again, there might be naysayers, but if a school district could show me evidence of significantly reduced truancy and tardiness, I would interpret this as a clear sign that positive things are happening in that district's classrooms.

A Summary of Recommendations

Because students' once-a-year scores on the currently available standardized achievement tests do not provide an accurate evaluation of instructional quality, educators must employ other (better) evidence-gathering approaches to assemble other (better) evidence. For individual teachers, I recommend the use of a split-and-switch data-gathering design so that students' responses can be blind-scored by teachers themselves or (preferably) by nonpartisans whose judgments will be seen by others as more believable.

For the evaluation of school-level or district-level instruction, I recommend a multifaceted strategy: Administrators must try to build a powerful case that, whether it leads to a positive or a negative judgment about the quality of instruction, will be credible to both the educators involved and the sometimes-skeptical external stakeholders and authorities.

I need to close this chapter with one final caution. We educators want to look good. Human beings are that way. But in a fevered quest for positive evidence about instructional quality, it's easy to forget the reason we ought to be evaluating instruction in the first place: to help kids learn better. Let's not get so caught up in the drive for rosy evaluations that we fail to identify instruction that needs to be improved. There's some poor instruction out there, and we need to get rid of it.

Wrapping Up
with Action Options

LET ME EXPLAIN WHY I'VE DECIDED TO CLOSE OUT THIS BOOK WITH A chapter about action *options*. Most people believe that options are good. Having a set of options gives us great freedom of choice: We can act or not act . . . do a lot or do a little.

As you may recall, way back in the Introduction, I explained that I hoped your reading of this book would accomplish two objectives. First, I wanted you to understand how the current misuses of unsound high-stakes tests can harm children educationally. Second, I wanted you to understand the features of an instructionally illuminating high-stakes test, so that you could distinguish between high-stakes tests that are educationally beneficial and those that are educationally destructive. If you walk away from this book having acquired this understanding, I'll be quite thrilled. But what I really want, and what the greater community of educators and school children really need, is for at least some of you to take action.

To Act or Not Act?

Your first option, of course, is to take no action related to what you've just finished reading. Maybe you'll bring to your own educational endeavors a deeper understanding of current assessment practice, sound and unsound testing, and ways to use tests to improve your own instruction. Should you participate in any sort of future dialogue about educational assessment, I'm confident that you'll be able to contribute better insights to the discussion. This is a nontrivial plus.

But maybe, just maybe, you might be inclined to try to do something to change what you regard as an unacceptable state of affairs regarding educational tests and how they're used these days. For those of you willing to take action, the remainder of this chapter sets out a whole range of action options for you to consider.

Before you make your big decision about whether to take action or not, let's be quite straightforward about what you may be secretly thinking. I'm assuming that most readers of this book are likely to be teachers or educational administrators. Some of those administrators will be highly placed and in an ideal position to influence the future of educational assessment in their school, district, or state. But those of you who are teachers or administrators with less pull may feel fairly powerless when it comes to taking the steps needed to make major changes in high-stakes testing programs.

I've talked to teachers all over the United States who, although dismayed by today's misuse of educational measurement, believe they can't do anything about it. I remember particularly one conversation with a 6th grade teacher in a midwestern state. "I understand what you're telling us about the harm that poor educational tests can cause," she told me, "but I can't do anything to fix it. After all, I'm just a classroom teacher!"

I've thought a good deal about this teacher's comment. I understand why she felt as she did, but I think she was flat-out wrong. I believe that every educator—yes, even classroom teachers—can contribute to the clean-up of today's educational measurement mess.

Start by sharing what you know. If you're a teacher, you might begin speaking out clearly and constructively whenever you take part in any conversations regarding educational testing. Whether it's a PTA meeting, a faculty meeting, or a chat with someone waiting in line at the grocery store, the constructive comments of a thoughtful teacher may be the spark that lights the fire that, in time, might burn out some of today's assessment silliness. Good ideas, cogently presented, can always make a difference.

Or let's say you're an assistant principal who routinely takes part in administrative consideration of such issues as "Improving our district's test scores" or "What kinds of test-preparation materials should we be buying?" You are in a great position to help your fellow administrators discard unsound assessment ideas and, instead, adopt assessment ideas that benefit students.

Generally speaking, an informed educator can dish out important measurement-related ideas to colleagues and noncolleagues alike. In time, those sensible assessment seeds may blossom. Don't underestimate the long-term effect that a reasonable set of assessment-related insights may have.

There are also opportunities for almost every educator to offer specific improvement-focused proposals to those who occupy positions of authority and have the clout to implement such proposals. You might prepare a one-page assessment-related proposal and submit it to a principal, to a district superintendent, or to a school board member. If the proposal has merit, it could lead to changes in the way educators and policymakers use tests. Having made it almost to the end of this book, you ought to be able to whip out several such proposals.

Transforming Chapters into Actions

My intent for this final chapter is to show those who are willing how to transform the information presented in this book into "make-things-better" action options. As you consider the following suggestions, I hope you'll come up with even better ideas about how you and your colleagues might take action to alter the educational mismeasurement that's rampant in our country.

Let me illustrate this point specifically. In Chapter 5, I described how to construct large-scale assessments (the kind that often become high-stakes tests) so that they are instructionally illuminating. I explained how a state or school district might go about building tests that will benefit children by helping teachers to make more defensible instructional decisions. If that kind of high-stakes test were used in your own locality (instead of, perhaps, a national standardized achievement test or a similarly functioning state-specific achievement test), high-stakes testing would help both teachers and students.

But, you may say, aren't such tests built by big companies' measurement specialists, and not by garden-variety educators? Yes, they are. But the measurement specialists who build national standardized achievement tests typically do so by contractually carrying out the specifications called for in an official request for proposal (RFP). An RFP is issued by state or district officials to the kinds of measurement companies that build high-stakes tests. In the RFP, the state and district officials explain their objectives for the new test and spell out very specific requirements for would-be contractors, such as how many items must be used per form, how many items must be created for each current standard to be assessed, how many forms of the test must be developed, and so on.

A variety of testing companies respond to the RFP by submitting proposals that explain how their company will meet the stated test requirements. A state or district review panel reviews all proposals, then decides which company will receive the contract to build the test. Test development is a business. Testing companies want to win these contracts so that they can make money and *stay* in business. And once awarded the contract, these companies will build *exactly the kind of test stipulated in the RFP.* Satisfied customers translate into future opportunities.

Largely because the architects of most assessment-related RFPs don't know any better, RFPs for statewide test-building have *not* required companies to build instructionally beneficial tests. Quite simply, some of the key requirements that must be stated if the resulting test is to benefit instruction are just not in those RFPs. For example, there are no requirements that the contractor create teacher-friendly assessment descriptions, or that the test's items be reviewed using an instructional perspective. Chapter 5's Rules 3 and 4 deal with this point. An instructionally *insensitive* RFP for a high-stakes test would never call for instructional guidelines for teachers, but might demand that all sorts of statistical gyrations be carried out on students' test scores. And *why* aren't these instructionally focused requirements typically included in RFPs for standardized achievement tests? Because no one has insisted on their inclusion. Do you see how you might fit into this equation?

Here's how it might work. You're a teacher who has decided to push for a more defensible high-stakes test in your state. You've re-read Chapter 5, and it's fresh in your mind that to be instructionally illuminating, a large-scale achievement test should contain the four features addressed in Chapter 5's four rules. By yourself, or in league with other teachers, you might simply write a letter to the state superintendent and copy each member of the state's board of education. In that letter you could urge the creation of a more instructionally beneficial high-stakes test, then identify several important elements that should be included in any RFP issued to build such a test.

I know full well that there are more potent political paths to travel if someone is trying to get a state's educational policymakers to undertake this sort of substantial test-development undertaking. But I'm trying to point out that *any* educator can contribute to the initiation of such a formidable and costly activity as the creation of a new high-stakes test—an activity apt to be seen as too massive by most educators. Remember, *you* don't have to build the instructionally spiffy statewide test; you only have to demand that *someone* build it.

An Array of Action Options

Although you do have the option of adopting a passive stance rather than taking an active role, please give at least a bit of thought to the following menu of activities. I believe that if many or all of these options were implemented during the next few years, we would see a dramatic reduction in the kinds of mismeasurement now eroding instructional quality in our schools. And, as a bonus, we'd start seeing greater use of large-scale and classroom assessments that contribute to improved instruction. Here, then, in no particular order of importance, are eight action options that you might have some interest in initiating or supporting.

Action Option 1: Offer Assessment Literacy Programs for All Teachers and Administrators.

As I've reiterated throughout this book, the U.S. educational community—with only a few exceptions—is not particularly conversant with the fundamentals of educational measurement. And I really do mean *fundamentals*. As with most specializations, it is possible to gussy-up educational measurement with all sorts of methodological regalia so that the topic will be intimidating to laypeople. But once you strip away all the technical trappings of educational assessment, the remaining core content is not terribly frightening.

What this first action option represents, then, is the installation of professional development programs dealing with the *essentials* of educational measurement, free from the quantitative quagmire. What all educators need to know to become assessment literate is not really overwhelming—and it won't take long for almost all educators in a district or a state to understand what they truly need to know about educational measurement.

Any sort of sensibly conceived, systematic staff development program about educational assessment should do the trick. I again urge you to take advantage of the plentiful, easy-to-understand books about educational testing that are available. I've listed several in the References and Resources section. In addition, there are quite a few first-rate videos about educational assessment on the market. In short, the resources your district or your school needs to promote educators' assessment literacy are already at hand. What is required is a commitment to create and deliver professional development programs that promote educators' assessment literacy.

Action Option 2: Provide Assessment Literacy Programs for Parents.

There are a lot of parents out there who are willing to take action to improve the quality of schooling their children receive. Indeed, much of the public agitation we see both for and against high-stakes tests stems increasingly from individual parents or organized groups of parents. But for the most part, parents of school-age children know even less about educational tests than do educators. This situation needs to be changed. Obviously, parents can be an enormously potent political force, and they can accomplish much good if they understand the issues involved. In the References and Resources, I've cited a couple of books about assessment written specifically for parents.

Of course, educators would be pretty silly to set up parent-focused assessment literacy programs without first carrying out Option 1 and promoting educators' assessment literacy. An assessment-literate group of educators can play a prominent role in getting more parents to understand what's *really* pivotal with respect to educational testing. In fact, I'd go so far as to discourage anyone from going ahead with Option 2 without first having implemented Option 1. I don't even want to contemplate the problems that would ensue in schools or school districts if parents knew lots more about educational testing than teachers and administrators!

As you're already beginning to see, certain of my suggested action options depend on the implementation of others. That's definitely the case with respect to Option 3, which depends absolutely on the implementation of Option 2's push for parental assessment literacy. And Option 2 depends on Option 1's implementation. Hmmm . . . are you sensing a pattern here?

Action Option 3: Establish Autonomous Parent-Action Groups.

As articulate (and accurate) as educators' public statements about the shortcomings of any high-stakes assessment program may be, there are some in the public realm who will be quick to discount or dismiss educators' viewpoints because of a perception of partisanship. We all know that there are people out there who think educators' complaints about any test-based accountability system are little more than whining by a flock of accountability phobic folks. (What we're somewhat more reluctant to admit is that in some instances, that perception is not too far from the truth.) But when *nonpartisans* speak up and point out the educational shortcomings of high-stakes testing programs, their criticisms are likely to be viewed as more credible. This is especially true when those nonpartisans are obviously assessment-literate.

Let's assume that a group of parents has become reasonably knowledgeable about educational testing and has received from educators an objective description of the local high-stakes testing program. At this point, the educators should disengage themselves from subsequent involvement with that group of parents. The assessment-literate parent group, having learned about the nature of a particular high-stakes program, may opt to do nothing.

But on the other hand . . . when assessment-knowledgeable parents learn about a local high-stakes testing program and see that it is likely to lower the quality of education their own children receive, many of those parents aren't going to sit still for it. In one way or another, they'll let the world know that something wrong is taking place.

What I want to stress, though, is that *if* the group of knowledgeable parents decides to take action—decides to express its displeasure with the assessment program to a local school board or a state legislator, for example—it should do so *autonomously*. All educators should be well out of the picture.

I realize some educators may be uneasy about fostering the creation of assessment-literate parent groups and then completely cutting ties with them. But because our objective is to make sure that the truth about ill-considered, educationally damaging high-stakes testing reaches policymakers, we need to make sure that well-informed parents who take up the cause cannot be discounted as the pawns of behind-the-scene educators.

Action Option 4: Offer Assessment-Related Briefing Sessions for Educational Policymakers.

Any group of assessment-literate educators should be able to put together a concise and informative explanatory session that will help busy educational policymakers understand the essential features of what seems to be wrong with an existing or proposed assessment system. The objective is to enhance the policymakers' understanding of local assessment issues. Better understanding will often (though not always) lead to better decisions.

Let's say the local school board has allotted you and your fellow educators 45 minutes on the agenda of an upcoming board meeting to present concerns about the district's high-stakes testing program. You'll need to devote great care to developing an honest, accurate, and persuasive briefing, complete with evidence to back up your analysis. (In Options 7 and 8, I'll suggest a pair of evidence-producing alternatives that you might consider.)

And your communication technique needs to be absolutely first-rate. Educational policymakers are almost always busy people; if you have a message to communicate to them, you've got to be quick about it. I've found that when working with policymakers, you can deliver your message much more effectively by using actual test items to illustrate your points. This tactic is far more powerful than presenting a litany of technical but abstruse assessment truths. Finally, if your analysis leads to a repudiation of the local high-stakes testing program, you must present ways of improving that program or ways of supplying alternative assessment-based data. Criticism unaccompanied by constructive alternatives is rarely persuasive.

Action Option 5: Initiate a Systematic Public Information Campaign Regarding Local High-Stakes Tests.

In recent years, I've spoken to far too many people on the street who unthinkingly equate students' test scores with the quality of schooling those students are receiving. The reason these people are so ill informed? By and large, the general populace relies on the media for information about national education issues. And I would say that most members of the media are unfamiliar with important issues involving educational tests.

Counter this perception by planning and implementing a meaningful public relations campaign. Designate individuals (or teams of individuals) to (1) write letters to the editors of local newspapers, (2) write lengthier op-ed essays for the same newspapers, and (3) conduct briefing sessions for the education writers or editorial staffs of those newspapers. In all three instances, your goal is to inform both laypeople and journalists about any potential problems that may exist in a local high-stakes testing program.

I have great confidence in the wisdom of an *informed* electorate. I have similar confidence in the activities of media personnel, as long as they know what's up. So this fifth item on the menu of action options essentially represents a systematic effort to smarten-up media folks and the public in general about educational assessment—and in particular about the virtues and vices of local high-stakes testing programs.

Action Option 6: Conduct Rigorous, Security-Monitored Reviews of the Items Found in a High-Stakes Test.

Reviewing the actual items in a high-stakes test is a path to enormous insight and the only means of determining what a high-stakes test is truly measuring. As you'll remember from Chapters 3 and 4, a superficial look at test items often gives the impression that items are appropriate, even when they're not. I advocate a deeper level of scrutiny, the kind of per-item scrutiny discussed in Chapter 5.

To conduct an item review, you'll need a review team, preferably comprising both educators and noneducators (to enhance the credibility of any judgments you issue). Getting access to sufficient copies of a high-stakes test used in your community can be a little tricky, as state assessment program staff tend to be reluctant to open up their high-stakes tests to outside scrutiny. In my experience, getting their cooperation is generally a matter of asserting the right kind of educational/political pressure. For the best results, I recommend having a group of assessment-literate parents lobby the state board of education and ask the state board to issue the request for an item review to the state assessment program staff.

Of course, reviews of items on high-stakes tests must be conducted under very strict security guidelines. All item reviews should take place under the supervision of a security monitor, charged with making sure that all distributed copies of the test have been returned and that no copy of the test ever leaves the item review room. I've run these sorts of monitored item review sessions many times in the past, and I'm confident that they can be conducted without compromising a test's security. Before anyone on your item review team sees Item 1, each reviewer should be required to sign an official nondisclosure agreement promising never to discuss, reveal, or reproduce from memory any items reviewed.

What should you and your review team look for when you consider each item? Each reviewer's primary objective should be to make per-item judgments that, when combined, will allow a third party to determine whether this test will add to or detract from children's education. The appropriate review criteria can vary from setting to setting, but the item review sample questions I listed in Chapter 5 provide a good starting point. If you remember, the evaluative dimensions these questions addressed were (1) curricular congruence, (2) instructional sensitivity, (3) presence of out-of-school factors, and (4) bias.

Following the completion of the item reviews, I recommend that the educators and noneducators on your review team report their judgments separately, not together. Such "disaggregated" reporting allows everyone to see how each of the two groups evaluated the test's items. When everything is complete, package your reports nicely and submit your findings to all relevant constituencies, including the media, the education committees of your state legislature, members of your district or state school board, and concerned organizations such as your school's PTA.

Action Option 7: Implement Defensible Evaluative Schemes for School- and District-Level Accountability.

I see nothing wrong with accountability-oriented programs for the evaluation of schooling *if these evaluations incorporate appropriate kinds of evidence.* It would be professionally and politically sense-

less to reject standardized achievement testing (an evaluative program that's based on the wrong data) without replacing it with a
new evaluative program that's based on the right data. Educators
need to set up and then implement new ways of more accurately
demonstrating that they have (or haven't) done a good job teaching
children. In short, Option 7 calls for the creation and implementation of an appropriate system of locally based educational accountability, rooted in rigorous and credible evaluative evidence.

In Chapter 7, I suggested how teachers and school administrators might collect believable evidence regarding their instructional
effectiveness. My suggestions focused not only on the use of relevant nontest indicators of a school's success, but also on the careful
pre-instruction to post-instruction gathering of both cognitive and
affective data from the same students. If you review Chapter 7, you'll
recognize what the adoption of this action option might involve. If
not gathered cautiously, locally collected evidence of educational
quality will be seen as self-serving applause by and for educators; it
won't be believed. For this reason, you must devote substantial attention to *how* any such evaluative evidence is garnered. Look over
the split-and-switch design's 12 steps and you'll see the sorts of pro-
cedural safeguards I have in mind.

I also believe that school staffs must be assisted, ideally by district or state authorities, in learning how to collect and succinctly report credible evidence about their success in promoting students'
mastery of important outcomes. Reports of such evidence, initially
provided at the school level (often in relation to a school's particular
improvement plan) and then (usually) aggregated at the district
level, can meaningfully buttress the kinds of accountability evidence
secured from other sources. What you can do to promote the use of
defensible evaluative models is to lobby for the provision of self-
development programs that give you and your colleagues the
know-how necessary to collect suitable evaluative data. Then, after
taking part in such self-development activities, you might take a
crack at developing a formal proposal for your school, district, or
state.

Action Option 8: Demand the Installation of a More Educationally Appropriate High-Stakes Statewide Test.

There will always be some citizens and policymakers who will approach "home-grown" tests with skepticism and insist on accountability evidence from "a major statewide test." Typically, a state will use one of two kinds of tests for state-level high-stakes assessment: a national standardized achievement test or a state-developed achievement test. But as we have discussed, many of today's state-customized tests have been built by the same companies that make the national tests. They've been constructed using the same traditional, score-spread–focused procedures that lead to the same problems explored in Chapters 3 and 4.

The only appealing alternative is to dump these bad tests and install good ones in their place. This eighth and final action option is for one or more educators to put together a persuasive position paper urging the development and issuance of an RFP that will call for the creation of an *instructionally sensible* accountability test.

In Chapter 5, I laid out the pivotal features of such a test. And earlier in this chapter, I went through why a focus on standardized test RFPs is an effective approach. With this book's information under your belt, it should not be difficult for you to create a position paper calling for an instructionally beneficial accountability test. All you need to do is urge key decision makers—especially elected executives and state legislators—to support the creation of credible accountability tests that help rather than harm students. Feel free to bolster your argument with some of the examples I've provided.

Tell the key decision makers in your state that it is definitely possible to build large-scale assessments that can measure instructional quality while providing appropriate clarification of the assessment program's targets. Tell them this clarification will help teachers direct their instruction toward the important bodies of knowledge and skills being measured, rather than toward the specific items on any particular test form.

Be prepared to deal with the reality of state education budgets. Tell your state officials that you realize the creation of a new, customized, instructionally illuminating test will *initially* cost more than simply using an off-the-shelf test. But stress that the test development cost will be trivial when contrasted with the profound educational calamities that accompany an accountability program relying on the wrong kind of high-stakes test.

Moreover, you might point out that most states could save a substantial chunk of money by reducing the number of poor assessments they are currently paying for. In certain states, national standardized achievement tests are now administered at *every* grade level from 3rd grade through 11th grade. Scaling back test administration to only two or three grades would still give state policymakers some evidence to use to compare their state's children to a national sample, and the resultant savings in test costs could be reinvested to support the creation of new, instructionally illuminating accountability tests designed specifically to assess a given state's curricular aspirations.

Choosing One, Some, All, or None

In the past decade, I've seen an enormous misuse of unsound high-stakes testing. And this expanding mismeasurement is leading to a deterioration of our children's education. Moreover, I see that both large-scale tests and classroom tests *could* produce potent instructional payoffs, if only those tests were fashioned with instruction in mind. Let me close this book, then, with a final plea.

If you share any of my perceptions about what's happening in U.S. education because of inadequate assessment, the harm that's being done, and the instructional dividends that are *not* being achieved, please do something about it. If you find yourself even slightly enticed by one or more of the options described in this chapter, I urge you to follow that inclination, heed this call to action, and make something happen. Each one of us can make a difference. I wish you the very best of luck.

References and Resources

Airasian, P. W. (1997). *Classroom assessment* (3rd ed.). New York: McGraw-Hill.

Anderson, L. W., & Bourke, S. F. (2000). *Assessing affective characteristics in the schools* (2nd ed.). Mahwah, NJ: Lawrence Erlbaum Associates.

Commonwealth of Virginia Board of Education. (1995). *Grade 4 standards of learning for Virginia public schools.* Richmond, VA: Author.

Florida Department of Education. (2001). *FCAT test item and performance task specifications, mathematics grades 9–10.* Tallahassee, FL: Author.

Freeman, D. J., Kuhs, T. M., Porter, A. C., Floden, R. E., Schmidt, W. H., & Schwille, J. R. (1984). Do textbooks and tests define a national curriculum in elementary school mathematics? *Elementary School Journal, 83*(5), 501–513.

Gardner, H. (1994). Multiple intelligences: The theory in practice. *Teachers College Record, 95*(4), 576–583.

Hawaii State Commission on Performance Standards. (1994). *1994 final report of the Hawaii State Commission on performance standards.* Honolulu, HI: Author.

Kohn, A. (2000). *The case against standardized testing: Raising the scores, ruining the schools.* Westport, CT: Heinemann.

Lemann, N. (1999). *The big test.* New York: Farrar, Straus, and Giroux.

Linn, R. L. (2000). Assessments and accountability. *Educational Researcher, 29*(2), 4–16.

McMillan, J. H. (2001). *Classroom assessment: Principles and practice for effective instruction* (2nd ed.). Boston: Allyn and Bacon.

Ohanian, S. (1999). *One size fits few.* Portsmouth, NH: Heinemann.

Popham, W. J. (1999). Where large-scale assessment is heading and why it shouldn't. *Educational Measurement: Issues and Practice, 18*(3), 13–17.

Popham, W. J. (2000a). *Modern educational measurement: Practical guidelines for educational leaders* (3rd ed.). Boston: Allyn and Bacon.

Popham, W. J. (2000b, December). Putting instruction on the line. *The School Administrator, 57*(11), 46–48.

Popham, W. J. (in press). *Classroom assessment: What teachers need to know* (3rd ed.). Boston: Allyn and Bacon.

Stiggins, R. J. (2001). *Student-involved classroom assessment* (3rd ed.). Upper Saddle River, NJ: Prentice-Hall.

U.S. Department of Agriculture (2000, April 27). *Expenditures on children by families*. Washington, DC: Author.

Here are two books about assessment written specifically for parents:

Popham, W. J. (2000). *Testing! testing! What every parent should know about school tests*. Boston: Allyn & Bacon.

Stiggins, R. J., & Knight, T. (1997). *But are they learning?* Portland, OR: Assessment Training Institute.

Assessment literacy videotapes are available from the following organizations:

Assessment Training Institute (ATI)
50 S.W. Second Avenue, Suite 300
Portland, OR 97204-2636
503-228-3060

Association for Supervision and Curriculum Development (ASCD)
1703 North Beauregard Street
Alexandria, VA 22311-1714
800-933-2723

IOX Assessment Associates
5301 Beethoven Street, Suite 190
Los Angeles, CA 90066
310-822-3275

Index

About the Author

W. JAMES POPHAM HAS SPENT THE BULK OF HIS EDUCATIONAL CAREER AS A teacher, first in a small, eastern Oregon high school, then in the UCLA Graduate School of Education and Information Studies. In his nearly 30 years at UCLA, Dr. Popham taught courses in instructional methods for prospective teachers and courses in evaluation and measurement for master's and doctoral candidates. He has won several distinguished teaching awards. In 1992, he took early retirement from UCLA (lured, he claims, by the promise of free parking for emeritus professors). In January 2000, he was recognized by *UCLA Today* as one of UCLA's top 20 professors of the 20th century.

Dr. Popham has written 20 books, 180 journal articles, 50 research reports, and 150 papers presented before research societies. In 1978, he was elected to the presidency of the American Educational Research Association (AERA). He was also the founding editor of *Educational Evaluation and Policy Analysis,* a quarterly journal published by AERA.

Related ASCD Resources:
High-Stakes Testing and Classroom Assessment

ASCD stock numbers are in parentheses.

Audiotapes

Are Standards and Accountability Improving Achievement or Inhibiting Instruction? by Leslie S. Kaplan and William A. Owings (#201201)

Educative Assessment: Building a State System Designed to Improve Learning by Samuel Houston and Grant Wiggins (#297048)

How State Standards are Helping—and Harming—Students and Schools by Christopher Cross, Susan O'Hanian, William Spady, and Grant Wiggins (#200144)

Promoting Parents' and Policymakers' Assessment Literacy by W. James Popham (#200106)

Purposeful Assessment by Mark Rosenbaum (#299204)

Using Classroom Assessment to Promote Student Learning by Lorrie Shepard (#299343)

Why Standardized Tests Can't Measure Educational Quality by W. James Popham (#200153)

Online Professional Development

Visit ASCD's Home Page (http://www.ascd.org) and click on Professional Development:

ASCD Online Member Benefits: Complete text of *Educational Leadership, ASCD Curriculum Update,* and *ASCD Education Update* (password protected)

ASCD Online Free Tutorial on *Performance Assessment*

Print Products

ASCD Infobrief 23 (November 2000): High-Stakes Tests (#101076)

Educational Leadership (March 1999): Using Standards and Assessment (#199027)

Great Performances: Creating Classroom-Based Assessment Tasks by Larry Lewin and Betty Jean Shoemaker (#198184)

A Practical Guide to Alternative Assessment by Pamela R. Aschbacher, Joan Herman, and Lynn Winters (#61192140)

Transforming Classroom Grading by Robert J. Marzano (#100053)

Videotapes

Developing Performance Assessments with Mary Kay Armour, Grant Wiggins, and Jay McTighe (#496251)

Redesigning Assessment Series: Introduction, Portfolios, Performance Assessment. (3-tape series with facilitator's guides; each tape also available separately) (#614237)

Professional Inquiry Kits

Assessing Student Performance by Judith A. Arther (#196214)

For additional resources, visit us on the World Wide Web (http://www.ascd.org), send an e-mail message to member@ascd.org, call the ASCD Service Center (1-800-933-ASCD or 703-578-9600, then press 2), send a fax to 703-575-5400, or write to Information Services, ASCD, 1703 N. Beauregard St., Alexandria, VA 22311-1714 USA.